The Book of Psalms

Psalms 01

¹ Blessed is the man who doesn't walk in the counsel of the wicked, Nor stand in the way of sinners, Nor sit in the seat of scoffers;
² But his delight is in the law of Yahweh; On his law he meditates day and night.
³ He shall be like a tree planted by the streams of water, That brings forth its fruit in its season, Whose leaf also does not wither. Whatever he does shall prosper.
⁴ The wicked are not so, But are like the chaff which the wind drives away.
⁵ Therefore the wicked shall not stand in the judgment, Nor sinners in the congregation of the righteous.
⁶ For Yahweh knows the way of the righteous, But the way of the wicked shall perish. Psalm 2

Psalms 02

¹ Why do the nations rage, And the peoples plot a vain thing?

2 The kings of the earth take a stand, And the rulers take counsel together, Against Yahweh, and against his anointed, saying,
3 "Let us break their bonds apart, And cast away their cords from us."
4 He who sits in the heavens will laugh. The Lord will have them in derision.
5 Then he will speak to them in his anger, And terrify them in his wrath:
6 "Yet I have set my king on my holy hill of Zion."
7 I will tell of the decree. Yahweh said to me, "You are my son. Today I have become your father.
8 Ask of me, and I will give the nations for your inheritance, The uttermost parts of the earth for your possession.
9 You shall break them with a rod of iron. You shall dash them in pieces like a potter's vessel."
10 Now therefore be wise, you kings. Be instructed, you judges of the earth.
11 Serve Yahweh with fear, And rejoice with trembling.
12 Kiss the son, lest he be angry, and you perish in the way, For his wrath will soon be kindled. Blessed are all those who take refuge in him. Psalm 3 A Psalm by David, when he fled from Absalom, his son.

Psalms 03

[1] Yahweh, how my adversaries have increased! Many are those who rise up against me.

[2] Many there are who say of my soul, There is no help for him in God. Selah.

[3] But you, Yahweh, are a shield around me, My glory, and the one who lifts up my head.

[4] I cry to Yahweh with my voice, And he answers me out of his holy hill. Selah.

[5] I laid myself down and slept. I awakened; for Yahweh sustains me.

[6] I will not be afraid of tens of thousands of people Who have set themselves against me on every side.

[7] Arise, Yahweh! Save me, my God! For you have struck all of my enemies on the cheek bone. You have broken the teeth of the wicked.

[8] Salvation belongs to Yahweh. Your blessing be on your people. Selah. Psalm 4 For the Chief Musician; on stringed instruments. A Psalm by David.

Psalms 04

¹ Answer me when I call, God of my righteousness. Give me relief from my distress. Have mercy on me, and hear my prayer.

² You sons of men, how long shall my glory be turned into dishonor? Will you love vanity, and seek after falsehood? Selah.
³ But know that Yahweh has set apart for himself him who is godly: Yahweh will hear when I call to him.
⁴ Stand in awe, and don`t sin. Search your own heart on your bed, and be still. Selah.
⁵ Offer the sacrifices of righteousness. Put your trust in Yahweh.
⁶ Many say, "Who will show us any good?" Yahweh, let the light of your face shine on us.
⁷ You have put gladness in my heart, More than when their grain and their new wine are increased.
⁸ In peace I will both lay myself down and sleep, For you, Yahweh alone, make me live in safety. Psalm 5 For the Chief Musician, with the flutes. A Psalm by David.

Psalms 05

¹ Give ear to my words, Yahweh. Consider my meditation.

² Listen to the voice of my cry, my King, and my God; For to you do I pray.
³ Yahweh, in the morning shall you hear my voice. In the morning I will lay my requests before you, and will watch expectantly.
⁴ For you are not a God who has pleasure in wickedness. Evil can't live with you.
⁵ The arrogant shall not stand in your sight. You hate all workers of iniquity.
⁶ You will destroy those who speak lies. Yahweh abhors the blood-thirsty and deceitful man.
⁷ But as for me, in the abundance of your lovingkindness I will come into your house: I will bow toward your holy temple in reverence of you.
⁸ Lead me, Yahweh, in your righteousness because of my enemies. Make your way straight before my face.
⁹ For there is no faithfulness in their mouth. Their inward part is destruction. Their throat is an open tomb. They flatter with their tongue.
¹⁰ Hold them guilty, God. Let them fall by their own counsels; Thrust them out in the multitude of their transgressions, For they have rebelled against you.
¹¹ But let all those who take refuge in you rejoice, Let them always shout for joy, because you defend them. Let them also who love your name be joyful in you.
¹² For you will bless the righteous. Yahweh, you will surround him with favor as with a shield. Psalm 6 For the

Chief Musician; on stringed instruments, upon the eight-stringed lyre. A Psalm by David.

Psalms 06

1 Yahweh, don`t rebuke me in your anger, Neither discipline me in your wrath.

2 Have mercy on me, Yahweh, for I am faint. Yahweh, heal me, for my bones are troubled.
3 My soul is also in great anguish. But you, Yahweh — how long?
4 Return, Yahweh. Deliver my soul, And save me for your lovingkindness` sake.
5 For in death there is no memory of you. In Sheol, who shall give you thanks?
6 I am weary with my groaning; Every night I flood my bed; I drench my couch with my tears.
7 My eye wastes away because of grief; It grows old because of all my adversaries.
8 Depart from me, all you workers of iniquity, For Yahweh has heard the voice of my weeping.
9 Yahweh has heard my supplication. Yahweh will receive my prayer.
10 May all my enemies be ashamed and dismayed. They shall turn back, they shall be disgraced suddenly. Psalm 7

A meditation by David, which he sang to Yahweh, concerning the words of Cush, the Benjamite.

Psalms 07

¹ Yahweh, my God, I take refuge in you. Save me from all those who pursue me, and deliver me,
² Lest they tear apart my soul like a lion, Rending it in pieces, while there is none to deliver.
³ Yahweh, my God, if I have done this, If there is iniquity in my hands,
⁴ If I have rewarded evil to him who was at peace with me (Yes, I have delivered him who without cause was my adversary),
⁵ Let the enemy pursue my soul, and overtake it; Yes, let him tread my life down to the earth, And lay my glory in the dust. Selah.
⁶ Arise, Yahweh, in your anger. Lift up yourself against the rage of my adversaries. Awake for me. You have commanded judgment.
⁷ Let the congregation of the peoples surround you. Rule over them on high.
⁸ Yahweh administers judgment to the peoples. Judge me, Yahweh, according to my righteousness, And to my integrity that is in me.
⁹ Oh let the wickedness of the wicked come to an end, But establish the righteous; Their minds and hearts are searched by the righteous God.

¹⁰ My shield is with God, Who saves the upright in heart.
¹¹ God is a righteous judge, Yes, a God who has indignation every day.
¹² If a man doesn't relent, he will sharpen his sword; He has bent and strung his bow.
¹³ He has also prepared for himself the instruments of death. He makes ready his flaming arrows.
¹⁴ Behold, he travails with iniquity; Yes, he has conceived mischief and brought forth falsehood.
¹⁵ He has dug a hole, And has fallen into the pit which he made.
¹⁶ The trouble he causes shall return to his own head. His violence shall come down on the crown of his own head.
¹⁷ I will give thanks to Yahweh according to his righteousness, And will sing praise to the name of Yahweh Most High. Psalm 8 For the Chief Musician; on an instrument of Gath. A Psalm by David.

Psalms 08

¹ Yahweh, our Lord, how majestic is your name in all the earth, Who has set your glory above the heavens!
² From the lips of babes and infants you have established strength, Because of your adversaries, that you might silence the enemy and the avenger.
³ When I consider your heavens, the work of your fingers, The moon and the stars, which you have ordained;

⁴ What is man, that you think of him? The son of man, that you care for him?
⁵ For you have made him a little lower than the angels, And crowned him with glory and honor.
⁶ You make him ruler over the works of your hands. You have put all things under his feet:
⁷ All sheep and oxen, Yes, and the animals of the field,
⁸ The birds of the sky, the fish of the sea, And whatever passes through the paths of the seas.
⁹ Yahweh, our Lord, How majestic is your name in all the earth! Psalm 9 For the Chief Musician. Set to "The Death of the Son." A Psalm by David.

Psalms 09

¹ I will give thanks to Yahweh with my whole heart. I will tell of all your marvelous works.
² I will be glad and rejoice in you. I will sing praise to your name, you Most High.
³ When my enemies turn back, They stumble and perish in your presence.
⁴ For you have maintained my right and my cause. You sit on the throne judging righteously.
⁵ You have rebuked the nations. You have destroyed the wicked. You have blotted out their name forever and ever.

⁶ The enemy is overtaken by endless ruin. The very memory of the cities which you have overthrown has perished.
⁷ But Yahweh reigns forever. He has prepared his throne for judgment.
⁸ He will judge the world in righteousness. He will administer judgment to the peoples in uprightness.
⁹ Yahweh will also be a high tower for the oppressed; A high tower in times of trouble.
¹⁰ Those who know your name will put their trust in you, For you, Yahweh, have not forsaken those who seek you.
¹¹ Sing praises to Yahweh, who dwells in Zion, And declare among the people what he has done.
¹² For he who avenges blood remembers them. He doesn`t forget the cry of the afflicted.
¹³ Have mercy on me, Yahweh. See my affliction by those who hate me, And lift me up from the gates of death;
¹⁴ That I may show forth all your praise. In the gates of the daughter of Zion I will rejoice in your salvation.
¹⁵ The nations have sunk down in the pit that they made; In the net which they hid, their own foot is taken.
¹⁶ Yahweh has made himself known. He has executed judgment. The wicked is snared by the work of his own hands. Meditation. Selah.
¹⁷ The wicked shall be turned back to Sheol, Even all the nations that forget God.
¹⁸ For the needy shall not always be forgotten, Nor the hope of the poor perish forever.
¹⁹ Arise, Yahweh! Don`t let man prevail. Let the nations be judged in your sight.

[20] Put them in fear, Yahweh. Let the nations know that they are only men. Selah. Psalm 10

Psalms 10

[1] Why do you stand far off, Yahweh? Why do you hide yourself in times of trouble?
[2] In arrogance, the wicked hunt down the weak; They are caught in the schemes that they devise.
[3] For the wicked boasts of his heart`s cravings, He blesses the greedy, and condemns Yahweh.
[4] The wicked, in the pride of his face, Has no room in his thoughts for God.
[5] His ways are prosperous at all times; He is haughty, and your laws are far from his sight: As for all his adversaries, he sneers at them.
[6] He says in his heart, "I shall not be shaken; For generations I shall have no trouble."
[7] His mouth is full of cursing, deceit, and oppression. Under his tongue is mischief and iniquity.
[8] He lies in wait near the villages. From ambushes, he murders the innocent. His eyes are secretly set against the helpless.
[9] He lurks in secret as a lion in his ambush. He lies in wait to catch the helpless. He catches the helpless, when he draws him in his net.
[10] The helpless are crushed, they collapse, They fall under his strength.

¹¹ He says in his heart, "God has forgotten. He hides his face. He will never see it."
¹² Arise, Yahweh! God, lift up your hand! Don`t forget the helpless.
¹³ Why does the wicked condemn God, And say in his heart, "God won`t call me into account?"
¹⁴ But you do see trouble and grief; You consider it to take it into your hand. You help the victim and the fatherless.
¹⁵ Break the arm of the wicked. As for the evil man, seek out his wickedness until you find none.
¹⁶ Yahweh is King forever and ever! The nations will perish out of his land.
¹⁷ Yahweh, you have heard the desire of the humble. You will prepare their heart. You will cause your ear to hear,
¹⁸ To judge the fatherless and the oppressed, That man who is of the earth may terrify no more. Psalm 11 For the Chief Musician. By David.

Psalms 11

¹ In Yahweh do I take refuge. How can you say to my soul, "Flee as a bird to your mountain!"
² For, behold, the wicked bend their bows. They set their arrows on the strings, That they may shoot in darkness at the upright in heart.
³ If the foundations are destroyed, What can the righteous do?

⁴ Yahweh is in his holy temple. Yahweh is on his throne in heaven. His eyes observe. His eyes examine the children of men.
⁵ Yahweh examines the righteous, But the wicked and him who loves violence his soul hates.
⁶ On the wicked he will rain blazing coals; Fire, sulfur, and scorching wind shall be the portion of their cup.
⁷ For Yahweh is righteous. He loves righteousness. The upright shall see his face. Psalm 12 For the Chief Musician; upon an eight-stringed lyre. A Psalm of David.

Psalms 12

¹ Help, Yahweh; for the godly man ceases. For the faithful fail from among the children of men.
² Everyone lies to his neighbor. With flattering lips, and with a double heart, do they speak.
³ May Yahweh cut off all flattering lips, And the tongue that boasts,
⁴ Who have said, "With our tongue will we prevail. Our lips are our own. Who is lord over us?"
⁵ "Because of the oppression of the weak and because of the groaning of the needy, I will now arise," says Yahweh; "I will set him in safety from those who malign him."
⁶ The words of Yahweh are flawless words, As silver refined in a clay furnace, purified seven times.

⁷ You will keep them, Yahweh, You will preserve them from this generation forever.
⁸ The wicked walk on every side, When what is vile is exalted among the sons of men. Psalm 13 For the Chief Musician. A Psalm by David.

Psalms 13

¹ How long, Yahweh? Will you forget me forever? How long will you hide your face from me?
² How long shall I take counsel in my soul, Having sorrow in my heart every day? How long shall my enemy triumph over me?
³ Behold, and answer me, Yahweh, my God. Give light to my eyes, lest I sleep in death;
⁴ Lest my enemy say, "I have prevailed against him;" Lest my adversaries rejoice when I fall.
⁵ But I trust in your lovingkindness. My heart rejoices in your salvation.
⁶ I will sing to Yahweh, Because he has been good to me. Psalm 14 For the Chief Musician. By David.

Psalms 14

¹ The fool has said in his heart, "There is no God." They are corrupt, they have done abominable works. There is none who does good.
² Yahweh looked down from heaven on the children of men, To see if there were any who did understand, Who did seek after God.
³ They have all gone aside; they have together become corrupt. There is none who does good, no, not one.
⁴ Have all the workers of iniquity no knowledge, Who eat up my people as they eat bread, And don't call on Yahweh?
⁵ There were they in great fear, For God is in the generation of the righteous.
⁶ You put to shame the counsel of the poor, Because Yahweh is his refuge.
⁷ Oh that the salvation of Israel would come out of Zion! When Yahweh restores the fortunes of his people, Then Jacob shall rejoice, and Israel shall be glad. Psalm 15 A Psalm by David.

Psalms 15

¹ Yahweh, who shall dwell in your sanctuary? Who shall live on your holy hill?
² He who walks blamelessly, does what is right, And speaks truth in his heart;
³ He who doesn't slander with his tongue, Nor does evil to his friend, Nor casts slurs against his fellow man;

⁴ In whose eyes a vile man is despised, But who honors those who fear Yahweh; He who keeps an oath even when it hurts, and doesn`t change;
⁵ He who doesn`t lend out his money for usury, Nor take a bribe against the innocent. He who does these things shall never be shaken. Psalm 16 A Poem by David.

Psalms 16

¹ Preserve me, God, for in you do I take refuge.
² My soul, you have said to Yahweh, "You are my Lord. Apart from you I have no good thing."
³ As for the saints who are in the earth, They are the excellent ones in whom is all my delight.
⁴ Their sorrows shall be multiplied who give gifts to another god. Their drink-offerings of blood I will not offer, Nor take their names on my lips.
⁵ Yahweh assigned my portion and my cup. You made my lot secure.
⁶ The lines have fallen to me in pleasant places. Yes, I have a good inheritance.
⁷ I will bless Yahweh, who has given me counsel. Yes, my heart instructs me in the night seasons.
⁸ I have set Yahweh always before me. Because he is at my right hand, I shall not be moved.

⁹ Therefore my heart is glad, and my tongue rejoices. My body shall also dwell in safety.
¹⁰ For you will not leave my soul in Sheol, Neither will you allow your holy one to see corruption.
¹¹ You will show me the path of life. In your presence is fullness of joy. In your right hand there are pleasures forevermore. Psalm 17 A Prayer by David.

Psalms 17

¹ Hear, Yahweh, my righteous plea; Give ear to my prayer, that doesn`t go out of deceitful lips.
² Let my sentence come forth from your presence; Let your eyes look on equity.
³ You have proved my heart; you have visited me in the night; You have tried me, and found nothing; I have resolved that my mouth shall not disobey.
⁴ As for the works of men, by the word of your lips I have kept myself from the ways of the violent.
⁵ My steps have held fast to your paths, My feet have not slipped.
⁶ I have called on you, for you will answer me, God: Turn your ear to me. Hear my speech.
⁷ Show your marvelous lovingkindness, You who save those who take refuge by your right hand from their enemies.
⁸ Keep me as the apple of your eye; Hide me under the shadow of your wings,

⁹ From the wicked who oppress me, My deadly enemies, who compass me about.
¹⁰ They close up their callous hearts. With their mouth they speak proudly.
¹¹ They have now surrounded us in our steps. They set their eyes to cast us down to the earth.
¹² He is like a lion that is greedy of his prey, As it were a young lion lurking in secret places.
¹³ Arise, Yahweh, Confront him, cast him down. Deliver my soul from the wicked by your sword;
¹⁴ From men by your hand, Yahweh, From men of the world, whose portion is in this life, Whose belly you fill with your treasure: They are satisfied with children, Leave the rest of their substance to their babes.
¹⁵ As for me, I shall see your face in righteousness; I shall be satisfied, when I awake, with seeing your form. Psalm 18 For the Chief Musician. By David, the servant of Yahweh, who spoke to Yahweh the words of this song in the day that Yahweh delivered him from the hand of all his enemies, and from the hand of Saul. He said,

Psalms 18

¹ I love you, Yahweh, my strength.
² Yahweh is my rock, and my fortress, and my deliverer; My God, my rock, in whom I will take refuge; My shield, and the horn of my salvation, my high tower.

³ I will call on Yahweh, who is worthy to be praised; So shall I be saved from my enemies.
⁴ The cords of death surrounded me. The floods of ungodliness made me afraid.
⁵ The cords of Sheol were round about me; The snares of death came on me.
⁶ In my distress I called on Yahweh, And cried to my God. He heard my voice out of his temple, My cry before him came into his ears.
⁷ Then the earth shook and trembled. The foundations also of the mountains quaked and were shaken, Because he was angry.
⁸ There went up a smoke out of his nostrils, Fire out of his mouth devoured; Coals were kindled by it.
⁹ He bowed the heavens also, and came down. Thick darkness was under his feet.
¹⁰ He rode on a cherub, and flew. Yes, he soared on the wings of the wind.
¹¹ He made darkness his hiding-place, his pavilion around him, Darkness of waters, thick clouds of the skies.
¹² At the brightness before him his thick clouds passed, Hailstones and coals of fire.
¹³ Yahweh also thundered in the sky, The Most High uttered his voice, Hailstones and coals of fire.
¹⁴ He sent out his arrows, and scattered them; Yes, lightnings manifold, and routed them.
¹⁵ Then the channels of waters appeared, The foundations of the world were laid bare, At your rebuke, Yahweh, At the blast of the breath of your nostrils.

16 He sent from on high. He took me. He drew me out of many waters.
17 He delivered me from my strong enemy, From those who hated me; for they were too mighty for me.
18 They came on me in the day of my calamity, But Yahweh was my support.
19 He brought me forth also into a large place. He delivered me, because he delighted in me.
20 Yahweh has rewarded me according to my righteousness. According to the cleanness of my hands has he recompensed me.
21 For I have kept the ways of Yahweh, And have not wickedly departed from my God.
22 For all his ordinances were before me. I didn`t put away his statutes from me.
23 I was also blameless with him. I kept myself from my iniquity.
24 Therefore has Yahweh recompensed me according to my righteousness, According to the cleanness of my hands in his eyesight.
25 With the merciful you will show yourself merciful. With the perfect man, you will show yourself perfect.
26 With the pure, you will show yourself pure. With the crooked you will show yourself shrewd.
27 For you will save the afflicted people, But the haughty eyes you will bring down.
28 For you will light my lamp. Yahweh, my God, will light up my darkness.
29 For by you, I advance through a troop. By my God, I leap over a wall.

30 As for God, his way is perfect. The word of Yahweh is tried. He is a shield to all those who take refuge in him.
31 For who is God, except Yahweh? Who is a rock, besides our God,
32 The God who arms me with strength, and makes my way perfect?
33 He makes my feet like hinds` feet, And sets me on my high places.
34 He teaches my hands to war; So that my arms bend a bow of bronze.
35 You have also given me the shield of your salvation. Your right hand sustains me. Your gentleness has made me great.
36 You have enlarged my steps under me, My feet have not slipped.
37 I will pursue my enemies, and overtake them. Neither will I turn again until they are consumed.
38 I will strike them through, so that they will not be able to rise. They shall fall under my feet.
39 For you have girded me with strength to the battle. You have subdued under me those who rose up against me.
40 You have also made my enemies turn their backs to me, That I might cut off those who hate me.
41 They cried, but there was none to save; Even to Yahweh, but he didn`t answer them.
42 Then I beat them small as the dust before the wind. I cast them out as the mire of the streets.
43 You have delivered me from the strivings of the people. You have made me the head of the nations. A people whom I have not known shall serve me.

⁴⁴ As soon as they hear of me they shall obey me. The foreigners shall submit themselves to me.
⁴⁵ The foreigners shall fade away, And shall come trembling out of their close places.
⁴⁶ Yahweh lives; and blessed be my rock. Exalted be the God of my salvation,
⁴⁷ Even the God who executes vengeance for me, And subdues peoples under me.
⁴⁸ He rescues me from my enemies. Yes, you lift me up above those who rise up against me. You deliver me from the violent man.
⁴⁹ Therefore I will give thanks to you, Yahweh, among the nations, And will sing praises to your name.
⁵⁰ He gives great deliverance to his king, And shows lovingkindness to his anointed, To David and to his seed, forevermore. Psalm 19 For the Chief Musician. A Psalm by David.

Psalms 19

¹ The heavens declare the glory of God. The expanse shows his handiwork.
² Day after day they pour forth speech, And night after night they display knowledge.
³ There is no speech nor language, Where their voice is not heard.

⁴ Their voice has gone out through all the earth, Their words to the end of the world. In them he has set a tent for the sun,
⁵ Which is as a bridegroom coming out of his chamber, Like a strong man rejoicing to run his course.
⁶ His going forth is from the end of the heavens, His circuit to the ends of it; There is nothing hid from the heat of it.
⁷ The law of Yahweh is perfect, restoring the soul. The testimony of Yahweh is sure, making wise the simple.
⁸ The precepts of Yahweh are right, rejoicing the heart. The commandment of Yahweh is pure, enlightening the eyes.
⁹ The fear of Yahweh is clean, enduring forever. The ordinances of Yahweh are true, and righteous altogether.
¹⁰ More to be desired are they than gold, yes, than much fine gold; Sweeter also than honey and the extract of the honeycomb.
¹¹ Moreover by them is your servant warned. In keeping them there is great reward.
¹² Who can discern his errors? Forgive me from hidden errors.
¹³ Keep back your servant also from presumptuous sins. Let them not have dominion over me. Then I will be upright, I will be blameless and innocent of great transgression.
¹⁴ Let the words of my mouth and the meditation of my heart Be acceptable in your sight, Yahweh, my rock, and my redeemer. Psalm 20 For the Chief Musician. A Psalm by David.

Psalms 20

¹ May Yahweh answer you in the day of trouble. May the name of the God of Jacob set you up on high,
² Send you help from the sanctuary, Grant you support from Zion,
³ Remember all your offerings, And accept your burnt-sacrifice. Selah.
⁴ May He grant you your heart`s desire, And fulfill all your counsel.
⁵ We will triumph in your salvation. In the name of our God we will set up our banners: Yahweh fulfill all your petitions.
⁶ Now I know that Yahweh saves his anointed. He will answer him from his holy heaven, With the saving strength of his right hand.
⁷ Some trust in chariots, and some in horses, But we trust the name of Yahweh our God.
⁸ They are bowed down and fallen, But we rise up, and stand upright.
⁹ Save, Yahweh; Let the King answer us when we call! Psalm 21 For the Chief Musician. A Psalm by David.

Psalms 21

¹ The king rejoices in your strength, Yahweh! How greatly he rejoices in your salvation!
² You have given him his heart's desire, And have not withheld the request of his lips. Selah.
³ For you meet him with the blessings of goodness; You set a crown of fine gold on his head.
⁴ He asked life of you, you gave it to him, Even length of days forever and ever.
⁵ His glory is great in your salvation. You lay honor and majesty on him.
⁶ For you make him most blessed forever. You make him glad with joy in your presence.
⁷ For the king trusts in Yahweh. Through the lovingkindness of the Most High, he shall not be moved.
⁸ Your hand will find out all of your enemies. Your right hand will find out those who hate you.
⁹ You will make them as a fiery furnace in the time of your anger. Yahweh will swallow them up in his wrath. The fire shall devour them.
¹⁰ You will destroy their descendants from the earth, Their posterity from among the children of men.
¹¹ For they intended evil against you. They plotted evil against you which cannot succeed.
¹² For you will make them turn their back, When you aim drawn bows at their face.

¹³ Be exalted, Yahweh, in your strength, So we will sing and praise your power. Psalm 22 For the Chief Musician; set to "The Doe of the Morning." A Psalm by David.

Psalms 22

¹ My God, my God, why have you forsaken me? Why are you so far from helping me, and from the words of my groaning?
² My God, I cry in the daytime, but you don`t answer; In the night season, and am not silent.
³ But you are holy, You who inhabit the praises of Israel.
⁴ Our fathers trusted in you. They trusted, and you delivered them.
⁵ They cried to you, and were delivered. They trusted in you, and were not put to shame.
⁶ But I am a worm, and no man; A reproach of men, and despised by the people.
⁷ All those who see me mock me. They insult me with their lips. They shake their heads, saying,
⁸ "He trusts in Yahweh; Let him deliver him; Let him rescue him, since he delights in him."
⁹ But you brought me out of the womb. You made me trust at my mother`s breasts.
¹⁰ I was thrown on you from my mother`s womb. You are my God since my mother bore me.

¹¹ Don`t be far from me, for trouble is near. For there is none to help.
¹² Many bulls have surrounded me. Strong bulls of Bashan have encircled me.
¹³ They open their mouths wide against me, Lions tearing prey and roaring.
¹⁴ I am poured out like water. All my bones are out of joint. My heart is like wax; It is melted within me.
¹⁵ My strength is dried up like a potsherd. My tongue sticks to the roof of my mouth. You have brought me into the dust of death.
¹⁶ For dogs have surrounded me. A company of evil-doers have enclosed me. They pierced my hands and my feet.
¹⁷ I can count all of my bones. They look and stare at me.
¹⁸ They divide my garments among them. They cast lots for my clothing.
¹⁹ But don`t be far off, Yahweh. You are my help: hurry to help me.
²⁰ Deliver my soul from the sword, My precious life from the power of the dog.
²¹ Save me from the lion`s mouth; Yes, from the horns of the wild oxen you have answered me.
²² I will declare your name to my brothers. In the midst of the assembly, will I praise you.
²³ You who fear Yahweh, praise him! All you descendants of Jacob, glorify him! Stand in awe of him, all you descendants of Israel!
²⁴ For he has not despised nor abhorred the affliction of the afflicted, Neither has he hid his face from him; But when he cried to him, he heard.

²⁵ Of you comes my praise in the great assembly. I will pay my vows before those who fear him.
²⁶ The humble shall eat and be satisfied. They shall praise Yahweh who seek after him. Let your hearts live forever.
²⁷ All the ends of the earth shall remember and turn to Yahweh. All the relatives of the nations shall worship before you.
²⁸ For the kingdom is Yahweh`s. He is the ruler over the nations.
²⁹ All the rich ones of the earth shall eat and worship. All those who go down to the dust shall bow before him, Even he who can`t keep his soul alive.
³⁰ Posterity shall serve him. Future generations shall be told about the Lord.
³¹ They shall come and shall declare his righteousness to a people that shall be born, For he has done it. Psalm 23 A Psalm by David.

Psalms 23

¹ Yahweh is my shepherd: I shall lack nothing.

² He makes me to lie down in green pastures. He leads me beside still waters.

³ He restores my soul. He guides me in the paths of righteousness for his name`s sake.

⁴ Even though I walk through the valley of the shadow of death, I will fear no evil, for you are with me. Your rod and your staff, they comfort me.
⁵ You prepare a table before me in the presence of my enemies. You have anointed my head with oil. My cup runs over.
⁶ Surely goodness and lovingkindness shall follow me all the days of my life, And I shall dwell in Yahweh's house forever. Psalm 24 A Psalm by David.

Psalms 24

¹ The earth is Yahweh's, with its fullness; The world, and those who dwell therein.
² For he has founded it on the seas, And established it on the floods.
³ Who may ascend to Yahweh's hill? Who may stand in his holy place?
⁴ He who has clean hands and a pure heart; Who has not lifted up his soul to falsehood, And has not sworn deceitfully.
⁵ He shall receive a blessing from Yahweh, Righteousness from the God of his salvation.
⁶ This is the generation of those who seek Him, Who seek your face — even Jacob. Selah.

⁷ Lift up your heads, you gates; Be lifted up, you everlasting doors: The King of glory will come in.
⁸ Who is the King of glory? Yahweh strong and mighty, Yahweh mighty in battle.
⁹ Lift up your heads, you gates; Yes, lift them up, you everlasting doors: The King of glory will come in.
¹⁰ Who is this King of glory? Yahweh of Hosts, He is the King of glory. Selah. Psalm 25 By David.

Psalms 25

¹ To you, Yahweh, do I lift up my soul.

² My God, in you have I trusted, Let me not be put to shame. Don`t let my enemies triumph over me.
³ Yes, no one who waits for you shall be put to shame. They shall be put to shame who deal treacherously without cause.
⁴ Show me your ways, Yahweh. Teach me your paths.
⁵ Guide me in your truth, and teach me, For you are the God of my salvation, I wait for you all day long.
⁶ Yahweh, remember your tender mercies and your lovingkindness, For they are from old times.
⁷ Don`t remember the sins of my youth, nor my transgressions. Remember me according to your lovingkindness, For your goodness` sake, Yahweh.

⁸ Good and upright is Yahweh, Therefore he will instruct sinners in the way.
⁹ He will guide the humble in justice. He will teach the humble his way.
¹⁰ All the paths of Yahweh are lovingkindness and truth To such as keep his covenant and his testimonies.
¹¹ For your name`s sake, Yahweh, Pardon my iniquity, for it is great.
¹² What man is he who fears Yahweh? He shall instruct him in the way that he shall choose.
¹³ His soul shall dwell at ease. His seed shall inherit the land.
¹⁴ The friendship of Yahweh is with those who fear him. He will show them his covenant.
¹⁵ My eyes are ever on Yahweh, For he will pluck my feet out of the net.
¹⁶ Turn to me, and have mercy on me, For I am desolate and afflicted.
¹⁷ The troubles of my heart are enlarged. Oh bring me out of my distresses.
¹⁸ Consider my affliction and my travail. Forgive all my sins.
¹⁹ Consider my enemies, for they are many. They hate me with cruel hatred.
²⁰ Oh keep my soul, and deliver me. Let me not be put to shame, for I take refuge in you.
²¹ Let integrity and uprightness preserve me, For I wait for you.
²² Redeem Israel, God, Out all of his troubles. Psalm 26 By David.

Psalms 26

¹ Judge me, Yahweh, for I have walked in my integrity. I have trusted also in Yahweh without wavering.
² Examine me, Yahweh, and prove me. Try my heart and my mind.
³ For your lovingkindness is before my eyes. I have walked in your truth.
⁴ I have not sat with deceitful men, Neither will I go in with hypocrites.
⁵ I hate the assembly of evil-doers, And will not sit with the wicked.
⁶ I will wash my hands in innocence, So I will go about your altar, Yahweh;
⁷ That I may make the voice of thanksgiving to be heard, And tell of all your wondrous works.
⁸ Yahweh, I love the habitation of your house, The place where your glory dwells.
⁹ Don`t gather my soul with sinners, Nor my life with bloodthirsty men;
¹⁰ In whose hands is wickedness, Their right hand is full of bribes.
¹¹ But as for me, I will walk in my integrity. Redeem me, and be merciful to me.
¹² My foot stands in an even place. In the congregations will I bless Yahweh. Psalm 27 By David.

Psalms 27

¹ Yahweh is my light and my salvation. Whom shall I fear? Yahweh is the strength of my life. Of whom shall I be afraid?
² When evil-doers came at me to eat up my flesh, Even my adversaries and my foes, they stumbled and fell.
³ Though a host should encamp against me, My heart shall not fear. Though war should rise against me, Even then I will be confident.
⁴ One thing have I asked of Yahweh, that will I seek after, That I may dwell in the house of Yahweh all the days of my life, To see the beauty of Yahweh, And to inquire in his temple.
⁵ For in the day of trouble he will keep me secretly in his pavilion. In the covert of his tent will he hide me. He will lift me up on a rock.
⁶ Now shall my head be lifted up above my enemies around me. I will offer sacrifices of joy in his tent. I will sing, yes, I will sing praises to Yahweh.
⁷ Hear, Yahweh, when I cry with my voice. Have mercy also on me, and answer me.
⁸ When you said, "Seek my face," My heart said to you, "I will seek your face, Yahweh."
⁹ Don`t hide your face from me. Don`t put your servant away in anger. You have been my help. Don`t abandon me, neither forsake me, God of my salvation.
¹⁰ When my father and my mother forsake me, Then Yahweh will take me up.

¹¹ Teach me your way, Yahweh. Lead me in a straight path, because of my enemies.
¹² Don't deliver me over to the desire of my adversaries, For false witnesses have risen up against me, Such as breathe out cruelty.
¹³ I am still confident of this: I will see the goodness of Yahweh in the land of the living.
¹⁴ Wait for Yahweh. Be strong, and let your heart take courage. Yes, wait for Yahweh. Psalm 28 By David.

Psalms 28

¹ To you, Yahweh, I call. My rock, don't be deaf to me; Lest, if you are silent to me, I would become like those who go down into the pit.
² Hear the voice of my petitions, when I cry to you, When I lift up my hands toward your Most Holy Place.
³ Don't draw me away with the wicked, With the workers of iniquity who speak peace with their neighbors, But mischief is in their hearts.
⁴ Give them according to their work, and according to the wickedness of their doings. Give them according to the operation of their hands. Bring back on them what they deserve.
⁵ Because they don't regard the works of Yahweh, Nor the operation of his hands, He will break them down and not build them up.

⁶ Blessed be Yahweh, Because he has heard the voice of my petitions.
⁷ Yahweh is my strength and my shield. My heart has trusted in him, and I am helped. Therefore my heart greatly rejoices. With my song I will thank him.
⁸ Yahweh is their strength. He is a stronghold of salvation to his anointed.
⁹ Save your people, and bless your inheritance. Be their shepherd also, and bear them up forever. Psalm 29 A Psalm by David.

Psalms 29

¹ Ascribe to Yahweh, you sons of the mighty, Ascribe to Yahweh glory and strength.
² Ascribe to Yahweh the glory due to his name. Worship Yahweh in holy array.
³ The voice of Yahweh is on the waters. The God of glory thunders, even Yahweh on many waters.
⁴ The voice of Yahweh is powerful. The voice of Yahweh is full of majesty.
⁵ The voice of Yahweh breaks the cedars. Yes, Yahweh breaks in pieces the cedars of Lebanon.
⁶ He makes them also to skip like a calf; Lebanon and Sirion like a young wild ox.
⁷ The voice of Yahweh strikes with flashes of lightning.
⁸ The voice of Yahweh shakes the wilderness. Yahweh shakes the wilderness of Kadesh.

⁹ The voice of Yahweh makes the deer calve, And strips the forests bare. In his temple everything says, "Glory!"
¹⁰ Yahweh sat enthroned at the Flood. Yes, Yahweh sits as King forever.
¹¹ Yahweh will give strength to his people. Yahweh will bless his people with peace. Psalm 30 A Psalm. A Song for the Dedication of the Temple. By David.

Psalms 30

¹ I will extol you, Yahweh, for you have raised me up, And have not made my foes to rejoice over me.
² Yahweh my God, I cried to you, and you have healed me.
³ Yahweh, you have brought up my soul from Sheol. You have kept me alive, that I should not go down to the pit.
⁴ Sing praise to Yahweh, you saints of his. Give thanks to his holy name.
⁵ For his anger is but for a moment; His favor is for a lifetime. Weeping may stay for the night, But joy comes in the morning.
⁶ As for me, I said in my prosperity, "I shall never be moved."
⁷ You, Yahweh, when you favored me, made my mountain to stand strong. But when you hid your face, I was troubled.
⁸ I cried to you, Yahweh. To Yahweh I made supplication:

⁹ "What profit is there in my destruction, if I go down to the pit? Shall the dust praise you? Shall it declare your truth?
¹⁰ Hear, Yahweh, and have mercy on me. Yahweh, be my helper."
¹¹ You have turned my mourning into dancing for me. You have removed my sackcloth, and clothed me with gladness,
¹² To the end that my heart may sing praise to you, and not be silent. Yahweh my God, I will give thanks to you forever. Psalm 31 For the Chief Musician. A Psalm by David.

Psalms 31

¹ In you, Yahweh, do I take refuge. Let me never be put to shame: Deliver me in your righteousness.
² Bow down your ear to me. Deliver me speedily. Be to me a strong rock, A house of defense to save me.
³ For you are my rock and my fortress, Therefore for your name's sake lead me and guide me.
⁴ Pluck me out of the net that they have laid secretly for me, For you are my stronghold.
⁵ Into your hand I commend my spirit. You redeem me, Yahweh, God of truth.
⁶ I hate those who regard lying vanities, But I trust in Yahweh.

⁷ I will be glad and rejoice in your lovingkindness, For you have seen my affliction. You have known my soul in adversities.

⁸ You have not shut me up into the hand of the enemy. You have set my feet in a large place.

⁹ Have mercy on me, Yahweh, for I am in distress. My eye, my soul, and my body waste away with grief.

¹⁰ For my life is spent with sorrow, My years with sighing. My strength fails because of my iniquity. My bones are wasted away.

¹¹ Because of all my adversaries I have become utterly contemptible to my neighbors, A fear to my acquaintances. Those who saw me on the street fled from me.

¹² I am forgotten from their hearts like a dead man. I am like broken pottery.

¹³ For I have heard the slander of many, terror on every side, While they conspire together against me, They plot to take away my life.

¹⁴ But I trust in you, Yahweh. I said, You are my God.

¹⁵ My times are in your hand. Deliver me from the hand of my enemies, and from those who persecute me.

¹⁶ Make your face to shine on your servant. Save me in your lovingkindness.

¹⁷ Let me not be put to shame, Yahweh, for I have called on you. Let the wicked be put to shame. Let them be silent in Sheol.

¹⁸ Let the lying lips be mute, Which speak against the righteous insolently, with pride and contempt.

[19] Oh how great is your goodness, Which you have laid up for those who fear you, Which you have worked for those who take refuge in you, Before the sons of men!
[20] In the covert of your presence will you hide them from the plotting of man. You will keep them secretly in a pavilion from the strife of tongues.
[21] Praise be to Yahweh, For he has showed me his marvelous lovingkindness in a strong city.
[22] As for me, I said in my haste, "I am cut off from before your eyes." Nevertheless you heard the voice of my petitions when I cried to you.
[23] Oh love Yahweh, all you his saints! Yahweh preserves the faithful, And pays back him who deals proudly in full.
[24] Be strong, and let your heart take courage, All you who hope in Yahweh. Psalm 32 By David. A contemplative psalm.

Psalms 32

[1] Blessed is he whose disobedience is forgiven, Whose sin is covered.
[2] Blessed is the man to whom Yahweh doesn't impute iniquity, In whose spirit there is no deceit.
[3] When I kept silence, my bones wasted away through my groaning all day long.
[4] For day and night your hand was heavy on me. My strength was sapped in the heat of summer. Selah.

⁵ I acknowledged my sin to you. I didn't hide my iniquity. I said, I will confess my transgressions to Yahweh, And you forgave the iniquity of my sin. Selah.
⁶ For this, let everyone that is godly pray to you in a time when you may be found. Surely when the great waters overflow, they shall not reach to him.
⁷ You are my hiding place. You will preserve me from trouble. You will surround me with songs of deliverance. Selah.
⁸ I will instruct you and teach you in the way which you shall go. I will counsel you with my eye on you.
⁹ Don't be like the horse, or like the mule, which have no understanding, Whose are controlled by bit and bridle, or else they will not come near to you.
¹⁰ Many sorrows shall be to the wicked, But he who trusts in Yahweh, lovingkindness shall surround him.
¹¹ Be glad in Yahweh, and rejoice, you righteous! Shout for joy, all you who are upright in heart! Psalm 33

Psalms 33

¹ Rejoice in Yahweh, you righteous! Praise is fitting for the upright.
² Give thanks to Yahweh with the lyre. Sing praises to him with the harp of ten strings.
³ Sing to him a new song. Play skillfully with a shout of joy!

4 For the word of Yahweh is right. All his work is done in faithfulness.
5 He loves righteousness and justice. The earth is full of the lovingkindness of Yahweh.
6 By the word of Yahweh were the heavens made, All the host of them by the breath of his mouth.
7 He gathers the waters of the sea together as a heap. He lays up the deeps in storehouses.
8 Let all the earth fear Yahweh. Let all the inhabitants of the world stand in awe of him.
9 For he spoke, and it was done. He commanded, and it stood firm.
10 Yahweh brings the counsel of the nations to nothing. He makes the thoughts of the peoples to be of no effect.
11 The counsel of Yahweh stands fast forever, The thoughts of his heart to all generations.
12 Blessed is the nation whose God is Yahweh, The people whom he has chosen for his own inheritance.
13 Yahweh looks from heaven. He sees all the sons of men.
14 From the place of his habitation he looks out on all the inhabitants of the earth.
15 He who fashions all of their hearts. He considers all of their works.
16 There is no king saved by the multitude of a host. A mighty man is not delivered by great strength.
17 A horse is a vain thing for safety, Neither does he deliver any by his great power.
18 Behold, the eye of Yahweh is on those who fear him, On those who hope in his lovingkindness;

¹⁹ To deliver their soul from death, To keep them alive in famine.
²⁰ Our soul has waited for Yahweh. He is our help and our shield.
²¹ For our heart shall rejoice in him, Because we have trusted in his holy name.
²² Let your lovingkindness be on us, Yahweh, Since we have hoped in you. Psalm 34 By David; when he pretended to be insane before Abimelech, who drove him away, and he departed.

Psalms 34

¹ I will bless Yahweh at all times. His praise will always be in my mouth.
² My soul shall boast in Yahweh. The humble shall hear of it, and be glad.
³ Oh magnify Yahweh with me. Let us exalt his name together.
⁴ I sought Yahweh, and he answered me, And delivered me from all my fears.
⁵ They looked to him, and were radiant. Their faces shall never be covered with shame.
⁶ This poor man cried, and Yahweh heard him, And saved him out of all his troubles.
⁷ The angel of Yahweh encamps round about those who fear him, And delivers them.

⁸ Oh taste and see that Yahweh is good. Blessed is the man who takes refuge in him.
⁹ Oh fear Yahweh, you his saints, For there is no lack with those who fear him.
¹⁰ The young lions do lack, and suffer hunger, But those who seek Yahweh shall not lack any good thing.
¹¹ Come, you children, listen to me. I will teach you the fear of Yahweh.
¹² Who is someone who desires life, And loves many days, that he may see good?
¹³ Keep your tongue from evil, And your lips from speaking lies.
¹⁴ Depart from evil, and do good. Seek peace, and pursue it.
¹⁵ The eyes of Yahweh are toward the righteous. His ears listen to their cry.
¹⁶ The face of Yahweh is against those who do evil, To cut off the memory of them from the earth.
¹⁷ The righteous cry, and Yahweh hears, And delivers them out of all their troubles.
¹⁸ Yahweh is near to those who have a broken heart, And saves those who have a crushed spirit.
¹⁹ Many are the afflictions of the righteous, But Yahweh delivers him out of them all.
²⁰ He protects all of his bones. Not one of them is broken.
²¹ Evil shall kill the wicked. Those who hate the righteous shall be condemned.
²² Yahweh redeems the soul of his servants. None of those who take refuge in him shall be condemned. Psalm 35 By David.

Psalms 35

¹ Contend, Yahweh, with those who contend with me. Fight against those who fight against me.
² Take hold of shield and buckler, And stand up for my help.
³ Draw out also the spear, and stop the way against those who pursue me. Tell my soul, "I am your salvation."
⁴ Let those who seek after my soul be put to shame and brought to dishonor. Let those who plot my ruin be turned back and confounded.
⁵ Let them be as chaff before the wind, The angel of Yahweh driving them on.
⁶ Let their way be dark and slippery, The angel of Yahweh pursuing them.
⁷ For without cause have they hid their net in a pit for me. Without cause have they dug a pit for my soul.
⁸ Let destruction come on him unawares. Let his net that he has hidden catch himself. Into that destruction let him fall.
⁹ My soul shall be joyful in Yahweh. It shall rejoice in his salvation.
¹⁰ All my bones shall say, "Yahweh, who is like you, Who delivers the poor from him who is too strong for him, Yes, the poor and the needy from him who robs him?"

¹¹ Unrighteous witnesses rise up. They ask me about things that I don`t know about.
¹² They reward me evil for good, To the bereaving of my soul.
¹³ But as for me, when they were sick, my clothing was sackcloth. I afflicted my soul with fasting. My prayer returned into my own bosom.
¹⁴ I behaved myself as though it had been my friend or my brother. I bowed down mourning, as one who mourns his mother.
¹⁵ But in my adversity, they rejoiced, and gathered themselves together. The attackers gathered themselves together against me, and I didn`t know it. They tore at me, and didn`t cease.
¹⁶ Like the profane mockers in feasts, They gnashed their teeth at me.
¹⁷ Lord, how long will you look on? Rescue my soul from their destruction, My precious life from the lions.
¹⁸ I will give you thanks in the great assembly. I will praise you among many people.
¹⁹ Don`t let those who are my enemies wrongfully rejoice over me; Neither let them wink with the eye who hate me without a cause.
²⁰ For they don`t speak peace, But they devise deceitful words against those who are quiet in the land.
²¹ Yes, they opened their mouth wide against me. They said, "Aha! Aha! Our eye has seen it!"
²² You have seen it, Yahweh. Don`t keep silent. Lord, don`t be far from me.

²³ Wake up! Rise up to defend me, my God! My Lord, contend for me!
²⁴ Vindicate me, Yahweh my God, according to your righteousness; Don`t let them gloat over me.
²⁵ Don`t let them say in their heart, "Aha! That`s the way we want it." Don`t let them say, "We have swallowed him up!"
²⁶ Let them be put to shame and confounded together who rejoice at my calamity. Let them be clothed with shame and dishonor who magnify themselves against me.
²⁷ Let them shout for joy and be glad, who favor my righteous cause. Yes, let them say continually, "Yahweh be magnified, Who has pleasure in the prosperity of his servant!"
²⁸ My tongue shall talk about your righteousness and about your praise all day long. Psalm 36 For the Chief Musician. By David, the servant of Yahweh.

Psalms 36

¹ An oracle is within my heart about the disobedience of the wicked: "There is no fear of God before his eyes."
² For he flatters himself in his own eyes, Too much to detect and hate his sin.
³ The words of his mouth are iniquity and deceit. He has ceased to be wise and to do good.
⁴ He plots iniquity on his bed. He sets himself in a way that is not good; He doesn`t abhor evil.

⁵ Your lovingkindness, Yahweh, is in the heavens. Your faithfulness reaches to the skies.
⁶ Your righteousness is like the mountains of God. Your judgments are a great deep. Yahweh, you preserve man and animal.
⁷ How precious is your lovingkindness, God! The children of men take refuge under the shadow of your wings.
⁸ They shall be abundantly satisfied with the abundance of your house. You will make them drink of the river of your pleasures.
⁹ For with you is the spring of life. In your light shall we see light.
¹⁰ Oh continue your lovingkindness to those who know you, Your righteousness to the upright in heart.
¹¹ Don`t let the foot of pride come against me. Don`t let the hand of the wicked drive me away.
¹² There the workers of iniquity are fallen. They are thrust down, and shall not be able to rise. Psalm 37 By David.

Psalms 37

¹ Don`t fret because of evil-doers, Neither be envious against those who work unrighteousness.
² For they shall soon be cut down like the grass, And wither like the green herb.
³ Trust in Yahweh, and do good. Dwell in the land, and enjoy safe pasture.

⁴ Also delight yourself in Yahweh, And he will give you the desires of your heart.

⁵ Commit your way to Yahweh. Trust also in him, and he will do this:

⁶ He will make your righteousness go forth as the light, And your justice as the noon day sun.

⁷ Rest in Yahweh, and wait patiently for him. Don't fret because of him who prospers in his way, Because of the man who makes wicked plots happen.

⁸ Cease from anger, and forsake wrath. Don't fret, it leads only to evildoing.

⁹ For evildoers shall be cut off, But those who wait for Yahweh, they shall inherit the land.

¹⁰ For yet a little while, and the wicked will be no more. Yes, though you look for his place, he isn't there.

¹¹ But the humble shall inherit the land, And shall delight themselves in the abundance of peace.

¹² The wicked plots against the just, And gnashes at him with his teeth.

¹³ The Lord will laugh at him, For he sees that his day is coming.

¹⁴ The wicked have drawn out the sword, and have bent their bow, To cast down the poor and needy, To kill those who are upright in the way.

¹⁵ Their sword shall enter into their own heart. Their bows shall be broken.

¹⁶ Better is a little that the righteous has, Than the abundance of many wicked.

¹⁷ For the arms of the wicked shall be broken, But Yahweh upholds the righteous.

¹⁸ Yahweh knows the days of the perfect. Their inheritance shall be forever.
¹⁹ They shall not be put to shame in the time of evil. In the days of famine they shall be satisfied.
²⁰ But the wicked shall perish. The enemies of Yahweh shall be like the beauty of the fields. They will vanish — Vanish like smoke.
²¹ The wicked borrow, and don`t pay back, But the righteous give generously.
²² For such as are blessed by him shall inherit the land. Those who are cursed by him shall be cut off.
²³ A man`s goings are established by Yahweh. He delights in his way.
²⁴ Though he stumble, he shall not fall, For Yahweh holds him up with his hand.
²⁵ I have been young, and now am old, Yet I have not seen the righteous forsaken, Nor his children begging for bread.
²⁶ All the day long he deals graciously, and lends. His seed is blessed.
²⁷ Depart from evil, and do good; Live securely forever.
²⁸ For Yahweh loves justice, And doesn`t forsake his saints. They are preserved forever, But the children of the wicked shall be cut off.
²⁹ The righteous shall inherit the land, And live in it forever.
³⁰ The mouth of the righteous talks of wisdom. His tongue speaks justice.
³¹ The law of his God is in his heart. None of his steps shall slide.

[32] The wicked watches the righteous, And seeks to kill him.
[33] Yahweh will not leave him in his hand, Nor condemn him when he is judged.
[34] Wait for Yahweh, and keep his way, And he will exalt you to inherit the land. When the wicked are cut off, you shall see it.
[35] I have seen the wicked in great power, Spreading himself like a green tree in its native soil.
[36] But he passed away, and, behold, he was not. Yes, I sought him, but he could not be found.
[37] Mark the perfect man, and see the upright, For there is a future for the man of peace.
[38] As for transgressors, they shall be destroyed together. The future of the wicked shall be cut off.
[39] But the salvation of the righteous is from Yahweh. He is their stronghold in the time of trouble.
[40] Yahweh helps them, and rescues them. He rescues them from the wicked, and saves them, Because they have taken refuge in him. Psalm 38 A Psalm by David, for a memorial.

Psalms 38

[1] Yahweh, don`t rebuke me in your wrath, Neither chasten me in your hot displeasure.
[2] For your arrows have pierced me, Your hand presses hard on me.

³ There is no soundness in my flesh because of your indignation, Neither is there any health in my bones because of my sin.
⁴ For my iniquities have gone over my head. As a heavy burden, they are too heavy for me.
⁵ My wounds are loathsome and corrupt, Because of my foolishness.
⁶ I am pained and bowed down greatly. I go mourning all the day long.
⁷ For my loins are filled with burning. There is no soundness in my flesh.
⁸ I am faint and severely bruised. I have groaned by reason of the anguish of my heart.
⁹ Lord, all my desire is before you. My groaning is not hidden from you.
¹⁰ My heart throbs. My strength fails me. As for the light of my eyes, it also is gone from me.
¹¹ My lovers and my friends stand aloof from my plague. My kinsmen stand afar off.
¹² They also who seek after my life lay snares. Those who seek my hurt speak mischievous things, And meditate deceits all day long.
¹³ But I, as a deaf man, don`t hear. I am as a mute man who doesn`t open his mouth.
¹⁴ Yes, I am as a man who doesn`t hear, In whose mouth are no reproofs.
¹⁵ For in you, Yahweh, do I hope. You will answer, Lord my God.
¹⁶ For I said, "Don`t let them gloat over me, Or exalt themselves over me when my foot slips."

17 For I am ready to fall. My pain is continually before me.
18 For I will declare my iniquity. I will be sorry for my sin.
19 But my enemies are vigorous and many. Those who hate me without reason are numerous.
20 They who also render evil for good are adversaries to me, Because I follow what is good.
21 Don't forsake me, Yahweh. My God, don't be far from me.
22 Hurry to help me, Lord, my salvation. Psalm 39 For the Chief Musician. For Jeduthun. A Psalm by David.

Psalms 39

1 I said, "I will watch my ways, so that I don't sin with my tongue. I will keep my mouth with a bridle while the wicked is before me."
2 I was mute with silence. I held my peace, even from good. My sorrow was stirred.
3 My heart was hot within me. While I meditated, the fire burned: I spoke with my tongue:
4 "Yahweh, make me to know my end, What is the measure of my days. Let me know how frail I am.
5 Behold, you have made my days handbreadths. My lifetime is as nothing before you. Surely every man stands as a breath." Selah.
6 "Surely every man walks like a shadow. Surely they busy themselves in vain. He heaps up, and doesn't know who shall gather.

⁷ Now, Lord, what do I wait for? My hope is in you.
⁸ Deliver me from all my transgressions. Don`t make me the reproach of the foolish.
⁹ I was mute, I didn`t open my mouth, Because you did it.
¹⁰ Remove your scourge away from me. I am overcome by the blow of your hand.
¹¹ When you rebuke and correct man for iniquity, You consume his wealth like a moth. Surely every man is but a breath." Selah.
¹² "Hear my prayer, Yahweh, and give ear to my cry. Don`t be silent at my tears. For I am a stranger with you, A sojourner, as all my fathers were.
¹³ Oh spare me, that I may recover strength, Before I go away, and be no more." Psalm 40 For the Chief Musician. A Psalm by David.

Psalms 40

¹ I waited patiently for Yahweh. He turned to me, and heard my cry.
² He brought me up also out of a horrible pit, out of the miry clay. He set my feet on a rock, and gave me a firm place to stand.
³ He has put a new song in my mouth, even praise to our God. Many shall see it, and fear, and shall trust in Yahweh.
⁴ Blessed is the man who makes Yahweh his trust, And doesn`t respect the proud, nor such as turn aside to lies.

⁵ Many, Yahweh, my God, are the wonderful works which you have done, And your thoughts which are toward us. They can't be set in order to you; If I would declare and speak of them, they are more than can be numbered.
⁶ Sacrifice and offering you didn't desire. My ears have you opened: Burnt offering and sin offering have you not required.
⁷ Then I said, "Behold, I have come. It is written about me in the book in the scroll.
⁸ I delight to do your will, my God. Yes, your law is within my heart."
⁹ I have proclaimed glad news of righteousness in the great assembly. Behold, I will not seal my lips, Yahweh, you know.
¹⁰ I have not hidden your righteousness within my heart. I have declared your faithfulness and your salvation. I have not concealed your lovingkindness and your truth from the great assembly.
¹¹ Don't withhold your tender mercies from me, Yahweh. Let your lovingkindness and your truth continually preserve me.
¹² For innumerable evils have surrounded me. My iniquities have overtaken me, so that I am not able to look up. They are more than the hairs of my head. My heart has failed me.
¹³ Be pleased, Yahweh, to deliver me. Hurry to help me, Yahweh.
¹⁴ Let them be put to shame and confounded together who seek after my soul to destroy it. Let them be turned

backward and brought to dishonor who delight in my hurt.
¹⁵ Let them be desolate by reason of their shame that tell me, "Aha! Aha!"
¹⁶ Let all those who seek you rejoice and be glad in you. Let such as love your salvation say continually, "Let Yahweh be exalted!"
¹⁷ But I am poor and needy; May the Lord think about me. You are my help and my deliverer. Don`t delay, my God.
Psalm 41 For the Chief Musician. A Psalm by David.

Psalms 41

¹ Blessed is he who considers the poor: Yahweh will deliver him in the day of evil.
² Yahweh will preserve him, and keep him alive, He shall be blessed on the earth, And he will not surrender him to the will of his enemies.
³ Yahweh will sustain him on his sickbed, And restore him from his bed of illness.
⁴ I said, " Yahweh, have mercy on me. Heal me, for I have sinned against you."
⁵ My enemies speak evil against me: "When will he die, and his name perish?"
⁶ If he come to see me, he speaks falsehood. His heart gathers iniquity to itself. When he goes abroad, he tells it.
⁷ All who hate me whisper together against me. They imagine the worst for me.

8 "An evil disease," they say, "has afflicted him. Now that he lies he shall rise up no more."

9 Yes, my own familiar friend, in whom I trusted, Who ate bread with me, Has lifted up his heel against me.

10 But you, Yahweh, have mercy on me, and raise me up, That I may repay them.

11 By this I know that you delight in me, Because my enemy doesn`t triumph over me.

12 As for me, you uphold me in my integrity, And set me in your presence forever.

13 Blessed be Yahweh, the God of Israel, From everlasting and to everlasting! Amen and amen. BOOK II Psalm 42 For the Chief Musician. A contemplation by the sons of Korah.

Psalms 42

1 As the deer pants for the water brooks, So pants my soul after you, God.

2 My soul thirsts for God, for the living God. When shall I come and appear before God?

3 My tears have been my food day and night, While they continually ask me, "Where is your God?"

4 These things I remember, and pour out my soul within me, How I used to go with the crowd, and led them to the

house of God, With the voice of joy and praise, a multitude keeping a holy day.

⁵ Why are you in despair, my soul? Why are you disturbed within me? Hope in God! For I shall still praise him for the saving help of his presence.

⁶ My God, my soul is in despair within me. Therefore I remember you from the land of the Jordan, The heights of Hermon, from the hill Mizar.

⁷ Deep calls to deep at the noise of your waterfalls. All your waves and your billows have swept over me.

⁸ Yahweh will command his lovingkindness in the daytime. In the night his song shall be with me: A prayer to the God of my life.

⁹ I will ask God, my rock, "Why have you forgotten me? Why do I go mourning because of the oppression of the enemy?"

¹⁰ As with a sword in my bones, my adversaries reproach me, While they continually ask me, "Where is your God?"

¹¹ Why are you in despair, my soul? Why are you disturbed within me? Hope in God! For I shall still praise him, The saving help of my countenance, and my God.
Psalm 43

Psalms 43

¹ Vindicate me, God, and plead my cause against an ungodly nation. Oh, deliver me from deceitful and wicked men.
² For you are the God of my strength. Why have you rejected me? Why do I go mourning because of the oppression of the enemy?
³ Oh, send out your light and your truth. Let them lead me. Let them bring me to your holy hill, To your tents.
⁴ Then I will go to the altar of God, To God, my exceeding joy. I will praise you on the harp, God, my God.
⁵ Why are you in despair, my soul? Why are you disturbed within me? Hope in God! For I shall still praise him, The saving help of my face, and my God. Psalm 44 For the Chief Musician. By the sons of Korah. A contemplative psalm.

Psalms 44

¹ We have heard with our ears, God; Our fathers have told us, What work you did in their days, In the days of old.
² You drove out the nations with your hand, But you planted them. You afflicted the peoples, But you spread them abroad.
³ For they didn't get the land in possession by their own sword, Neither did their own arm save them; But your

right hand, and your arm, and the light of your face,
Because you were favorable to them.
⁴ You are my King, God. Command victories for Jacob!
⁵ Through you, will we push down our adversaries. Through your name, will we tread them under who rise up against us.
⁶ For I will not trust in my bow, Neither shall my sword save me.
⁷ But you have saved us from our adversaries, And have put them to shame who hate us.
⁸ In God have we made our boast all day long, We will give thanks to your name forever. Selah.
⁹ But now you rejected us, and brought us to dishonor, And don`t go out with our armies.
¹⁰ You make us turn back from the adversary. Those who hate us take spoil for themselves.
¹¹ You have made us like sheep for food, And have scattered us among the nations.
¹² You sell your people for nothing, And have gained nothing from their sale.
¹³ You make us a reproach to our neighbors, A scoffing and a derision to those who are round about us.
¹⁴ You make us a byword among the nations, A shaking of the head among the peoples.
¹⁵ All day long is my dishonor before me, And shame covers my face,
¹⁶ At the taunt of one who reproaches and reviles, Because of the enemy and the avenger.
¹⁷ All this has come on us, Yet have we not forgotten you, Neither have we been false to your covenant.

18 Our heart has not turned back, Neither have our steps declined from your way,
19 That you have crushed us in the haunt of jackals, And covered us with the shadow of death.
20 If we have forgotten the name of our God, Or spread forth our hands to a strange god;
21 Won`t God search this out? For he knows the secrets of the heart.
22 Yes, for your sake are we killed all day long. We are regarded as sheep for the slaughter.
23 Wake up! Why do you sleep, Lord? Arise! Don`t reject us forever.
24 Why do you hide your face, And forget our affliction and our oppression?
25 For our soul is bowed down to the dust. Our body cleaves to the earth.
26 Rise up to help us. Redeem us for your lovingkindness` sake. Psalm 45 For the Chief Musician. Set to "The Lilies." A contemplation by the sons of Korah. A wedding song.

Psalms 45

1 My heart overflows with a noble theme. I recite my verses for the king. My tongue is like the pen of a skillful writer.
2 You are the most excellent of the sons of men. Grace has anointed your lips, Therefore God has blessed you forever.

³ Gird your sword on your thigh, mighty one, Your splendor and your majesty.
⁴ In your majesty ride on victoriously on behalf of truth, humility, and righteousness. Let your right hand display awesome deeds.
⁵ Your arrows are sharp. The nations fall under you, with arrows in the heart of the king's enemies.
⁶ Your throne, God, is forever and ever. A scepter of equity is the scepter of your kingdom.
⁷ You have loved righteousness, and hated wickedness. Therefore God, your God, has anointed you with the oil of gladness above your fellows.
⁸ All your garments smell like myrrh, aloes, and cassia. Out of ivory palaces stringed instruments have made you glad.
⁹ Kings' daughters are among your honorable women. At your right hand the queen stands in gold of Ophir.
¹⁰ Listen, daughter, consider, and turn your ear. Forget your own people, and also your father's house.
¹¹ So will the king desire your beauty, Honor him, for he is your lord.
¹² The daughter of Tyre comes with a gift. The rich among the people entreat your favor.
¹³ The princess inside is all glorious. Her clothing is interwoven with gold.
¹⁴ She shall be led to the king in embroidered work. The virgins, her companions who follow her, shall be brought to you.
¹⁵ With gladness and rejoicing shall they be led. They shall enter into the king's palace.

¹⁶ Your sons will take the place of your fathers. You shall make them princes in all the earth.
¹⁷ I will make your name to be remembered in all generations. Therefore the peoples shall give you thanks forever and ever. Psalm 46 For the Chief Musician. By the sons of Korah. A song for Alamoth.

Psalms 46

¹ God is our refuge and strength, A very present help in trouble.
² Therefore will we not be afraid, though the earth changes, Though the mountains are shaken into the heart of the seas;
³ Though the waters of it roar and are troubled, Though the mountains tremble with the swelling of it. Selah.
⁴ There is a river, the streams of which make the city of God glad, The holy place of the tents of the Most High.
⁵ God is in the midst of her. She shall not be moved. God will help her at dawn.
⁶ The nations raged. The kingdoms were moved. He uttered his voice, and the earth melted.
⁷ Yahweh of Hosts is with us. The God of Jacob is our refuge. Selah.
⁸ Come, see the works of Yahweh, What desolations he has made in the earth.

⁹ He makes wars cease to the end of the earth. He breaks the bow, and cuts the spear apart. He burns the chariots in the fire.
¹⁰ "Be still, and know that I am God. I will be exalted among the nations. I will be exalted in the earth."
¹¹ Yahweh of Hosts is with us. The God of Jacob is our refuge. Selah. Psalm 47 For the Chief Musician. A Psalm by the sons of Korah.

Psalms 47

¹ Oh clap your hands, all you nations. Shout to God with the voice of triumph!
² For Yahweh Most High is awesome. He is a great King over all the earth.
³ He subdues nations under us, And peoples under our feet.
⁴ He chooses our inheritance for us, The glory of Jacob whom he loved. Selah.
⁵ God has gone up with a shout, Yahweh with the sound of a trumpet.
⁶ Sing praise to God, sing praises. Sing praises to our King, sing praises.
⁷ For God is the King of all the earth. Sing praises with understanding.
⁸ God reigns over the nations. God sits on his holy throne.
⁹ The princes of the peoples are gathered together, The people of the God of Abraham. For the shields of the

earth belong to God. He is greatly exalted! Psalm 48 A Song. A Psalm by the sons of Korah.

Psalms 48

¹ Great is Yahweh, and greatly to be praised, In the city of our God, in his holy mountain.
² Beautiful in elevation, the joy of the whole earth, Is Mount Zion, on the north sides, The city of the great King.
³ God has shown himself in her citadels as a refuge.
⁴ For, behold, the kings assembled themselves, They passed by together.
⁵ They saw it, then were they amazed. They were dismayed, They hurried away.
⁶ Trembling took hold of them there, Pain, as of a woman in travail.
⁷ With the east wind, you break the ships of Tarshish.
⁸ As we have heard, so have we seen, In the city of Yahweh of Hosts, in the city of our God. God will establish it forever. Selah.
⁹ We have thought about your lovingkindness, God, In the midst of your temple.
¹⁰ As is your name, God, So is your praise to the ends of the earth. Your right hand is full of righteousness.
¹¹ Let Mount Zion be glad! Let the daughters of Judah rejoice, Because of your judgments.

12 Walk about Zion, and go around her. Number the towers of it;
13 Mark well her bulwarks. Consider her palaces, That you may tell it to the next generation.
14 For this God is our God forever and ever. He will be our guide even to death. Psalm 49 For the Chief Musician. A Psalm by the sons of Korah.

Psalms 49

1 Hear this, all you peoples. Listen, all you inhabitants of the world,
2 Both low and high, Rich and poor together.
3 My mouth will speak words of wisdom. My heart shall utter understanding.
4 I will incline my ear to a proverb. I will open my riddle on the harp.
5 Why should I fear in the days of evil, When iniquity at my heels surrounds me?
6 Those who trust in their wealth, And boast in the multitude of their riches —
7 None of them can by any means redeem his brother, Nor give God a ransom for him.
8 For the redemption of their life is costly, No payment is ever enough,
9 That he should live on forever, That he should not see corruption.

¹⁰ For he sees that wise men die; Likewise the fool and the senseless perish, And leave their wealth to others.
¹¹ Their inward thought is, that their houses endure forever, And their dwelling places to all generations. They call their lands after their own names.
¹² But man, despite his riches, doesn't endure. He is like the animals that perish.
¹³ This is the destiny of those who are foolish, And of those who approve their sayings. Selah.
¹⁴ They are appointed as a flock for Sheol. Death shall be their shepherd. The upright shall have dominion over them in the morning. Their beauty shall be for Sheol to consume, That there be no habitation for it.
¹⁵ But God will redeem my soul from the power of Sheol, For he will receive me. Selah.
¹⁶ Don't be afraid when a man is made rich, When the glory of his house is increased.
¹⁷ For when he dies he shall carry nothing away. His glory shall not descend after him.
¹⁸ Though while he lived he blessed his soul — And men praise you when you do well for yourself —
¹⁹ He shall go to the generation of his fathers. They shall never see the light.
²⁰ A man who has riches without understanding, Is like the animals that perish. Psalm 50 A Psalm by Asaph.

Psalms 50

¹ The Mighty One, God, Yahweh, speaks, And calls the earth from sunrise to sunset.

² Out of Zion, the perfection of beauty, God shines forth.
³ Our God comes, and does not keep silence. A fire devours before him. It is very tempestuous around him.
⁴ He calls to the heavens above, To the earth, that he may judge his people:
⁵ "Gather my saints together to me, Those who have made a covenant with me by sacrifice."
⁶ The heavens shall declare his righteousness, For God himself is judge. Selah.
⁷ "Hear, my people, and I will speak; Israel, and I will testify against you. I am God, your God.
⁸ I don`t rebuke you for your sacrifices. Your burnt offerings are continually before me.
⁹ I have no need for a bull from your stall, Nor male goats from your pens.
¹⁰ For every animal of the forest is mine, And the cattle on a thousand hills.
¹¹ I know all the birds of the mountains. The wild animals of the field are mine.
¹² If I were hungry, I would not tell you, For the world is mine, and all that is in it.
¹³ Will I eat the flesh of bulls, Or drink the blood of goats?
¹⁴ Offer to God the sacrifice of thanksgiving. Pay your vows to the Most High.
¹⁵ Call on me in the day of trouble. I will deliver you, and you will honor me."
¹⁶ But to the wicked God says, "What right do you have to declare my statutes, That you have taken my covenant on your lips,

¹⁷ Seeing you hate instruction, And throw my words behind you?
¹⁸ When you saw a thief, you consented with him, And have participated with adulterers.
¹⁹ "You give your mouth to evil. Your tongue harnesses deceit.
²⁰ You sit and speak against your brother. You slander your own mother`s son.
²¹ You have done these things, and I kept silence. You thought that the "I AM" was just like you. I will rebuke you, and accuse you in front of your eyes.
²² "Now consider this, you who forget God, Lest I tear you in pieces, and there be none to deliver.
²³ Whoever offers the sacrifice of thanksgiving glorifies me, And prepares his way so that I will show God`s salvation to him." Psalm 51 For the Chief Musician. A Psalm by David, when Nathan the prophet came to him, after he had gone in to Bathsheba.

Psalms 51

¹ Have mercy on me, God, according to your lovingkindness. According to the multitude of your tender mercies, blot out my transgressions.
² Wash me thoroughly from my iniquity. Cleanse me from my sin.

3 For I know my transgressions. My sin is constantly before me.
4 Against you, and you only, have I sinned, And done that which is evil in your sight; That you may be proved right when you speak, And justified when you judge.
5 Behold, I was brought forth in iniquity. In sin did my mother conceive me.
6 Behold, you desire truth in the inward parts. You teach me wisdom in the inmost place.
7 Purify me with hyssop, and I will be clean. Wash me, and I will be whiter than snow.
8 Let me hear joy and gladness, That the bones which you have broken may rejoice.
9 Hide your face from my sins, And blot out all of my iniquities.
10 Create in me a clean heart, God. Renew a right spirit within me.
11 Don`t throw me away from your presence. Don`t take your holy Spirit from me.
12 Restore to me the joy of your salvation. Uphold me with a willing spirit.
13 Then I will teach transgressors your ways. Sinners shall be converted to you.
14 Deliver me from bloodguiltiness, God, you God of my salvation. My tongue shall sing aloud of your righteousness.
15 Lord, open my lips. My mouth shall declare your praise.
16 For you don`t delight in sacrifice, or else I would give it. You have no pleasure in burnt offering.

¹⁷ The sacrifices of God are a broken spirit. A broken and contrite heart, God, you will not despise.
¹⁸ Do well in your good pleasure to Zion. Build the walls of Jerusalem.
¹⁹ Then will you delight in the sacrifices of righteousness, In burnt offerings and in whole burnt offerings. Then they will offer bulls on your altar. Psalm 52 For the Chief Musician. A contemplation by David, when Doeg the Edomite came and told Saul, "David has come to Abimelech`s house."

Psalms 52

¹ Why do you boast of mischief, mighty man? God`s lovingkindness endures continually.
² Your tongue plots destruction, Like a sharp razor, working deceitfully.
³ You love evil more than good, Lying rather than speaking the truth. Selah.
⁴ You love all devouring words, You deceitful tongue.
⁵ God will likewise destroy you forever. He will take you up, and pluck you out of your tent, And root you out of the land of the living. Selah.
⁶ The righteous also will see it, and fear, And laugh at him, saying,
⁷ "Behold, this is the man who didn`t make God his strength, But trusted in the abundance of his riches, And strengthened himself in his wickedness."

8 But as for me, I am like a green olive tree in God's house. I trust in God's lovingkindness forever and ever.
9 I will give you thanks forever, because you have done it. I will hope in your name, for it is good, In the presence of your saints. Psalm 53 For the Chief Musician. To the tune of "Mahalath." A contemplation by David.

Psalms 53

1 The fool has said in his heart, "There is no God." They are corrupt, and have done abominable iniquity. There is no one who does good.
2 God looks down from heaven on the children of men, To see if there are any who understood, Who seek after God.
3 Every one of them has gone back. They have become filthy together. There is no one who does good, no, not one.
4 Have the workers of iniquity no knowledge, Who eat up my people as they eat bread, And don't call on God?
5 There they were in great fear, where no fear was, For God has scattered the bones of him who encamps against you. You have put them to shame, Because God has rejected them.
6 Oh that the salvation of Israel had already come out of Zion! When God brings back the captivity of his people, Then shall Jacob rejoice. Israel shall be glad. Psalm 54 For the Chief Musician. On stringed instruments. A contemplation by David, when the Ziphites came and said to Saul, "Isn't David hiding himself among us?"

Psalms 54

¹ Save me, God, by your name. Vindicate me in your might.
² Hear my prayer, God. Listen to the words of my mouth.
³ For strangers have risen up against me. Violent men have sought after my soul. They haven`t set God before them. Selah.
⁴ Behold, God is my helper. The Lord is the one who sustains my soul.
⁵ He will repay the evil to my enemies. Destroy them in your truth.
⁶ With a free will offering, I will sacrifice to you. I will give thanks to your name, Yahweh, for it is good.
⁷ For he has delivered me out of all trouble. My eye has seen triumph over my enemies. Psalm 55 For the Chief Musician. On stringed instruments. A contemplation by David.

Psalms 55

¹ Listen to my prayer, God. Don`t hide yourself from my supplication.
² Attend to me, and answer me. I am restless in my complaint, and moan,

³ Because of the voice of the enemy, Because of the oppression of the wicked. For they bring suffering on me. In anger they hold a grudge against me.
⁴ My heart is severely pained within me. The terrors of death have fallen on me.
⁵ Fearfulness and trembling have come on me. Horror has overwhelmed me.
⁶ I said, "Oh that I had wings like a dove! Then I would fly away, and be at rest.
⁷ Behold, then I would wander far off. I would lodge in the wilderness." Selah.
⁸ "I would hurry to a shelter from the stormy wind and tempest."
⁹ Confuse them, Lord, and confound their language, For I have seen violence and strife in the city.
¹⁰ Day and night they prowl around on its walls. Malice and abuse are also within her.
¹¹ Destructive forces are within her. Threats and lies don`t depart from her streets.
¹² For it was not an enemy who insulted me, Then I could have endured it. Neither was it he who hated me who raised himself up against me, Then I would have hid myself from him.
¹³ But it was you, a man like me, My companion, and my familiar friend.
¹⁴ We took sweet fellowship together. We walked in God`s house with the throng.
¹⁵ Let death come suddenly on them. Let them go down alive into Sheol. For wickedness is in their dwelling, in the midst of them.

16 As for me, I will call on God. Yahweh will save me.
17 Evening, morning, and at noon, I will cry out in distress. He will hear my voice.
18 He has redeemed my soul in peace from the battle that was against me, Although there are many who oppose me.
19 God, who is enthroned forever, Will hear, and answer them. Selah. They never change, Who don`t fear God.
20 He raises his hands against his friends. He has violated his covenant.
21 His mouth was smooth as butter, But his heart was war. His words were softer than oil, Yet they were drawn swords.
22 Cast your burden on Yahweh, and he will sustain you. He will never allow the righteous to be moved.
23 But you, God, will bring them down into the pit of destruction. Bloodthirsty and deceitful men shall not live out half their days, But I will trust in you. Psalm 56 For the Chief Musician. To the tune of "Silent Dove in Distant Lands". A poem by David, when the Philistines seized him in Gath.

Psalms 56

1 Be merciful to me, God, for man wants to swallow me up. All day long, he attacks and oppresses me.

² My enemies want to swallow me up all day long, For they are many who fight proudly against me.
³ When I am afraid, I will put my trust in you.
⁴ In God, I praise his word. In God, I put my trust. I will not be afraid. What can flesh do to me?
⁵ All day long they twist my words. All their thoughts are against me for evil.
⁶ They conspire and lurk, Watching my steps, they are eager to take my life.
⁷ Shall they escape by iniquity? In anger cast down the peoples, God.
⁸ You number my wanderings. You put my tears into your bottle. Aren`t they in your book?
⁹ Then shall my enemies turn back in the day that I call. I know this, that God is for me.
¹⁰ In God, I will praise his word. In Yahweh, I will praise his word.
¹¹ I have put my trust in God. I will not be afraid. What can man do to me?
¹² Your vows are on me, God. I will give thank offerings to you.
¹³ For you have delivered my soul from death, And prevented my feet from falling, That I may walk before God in the light of the living. Psalm 57 For the Chief Musician. To the tune of "Do Not Destroy." A poem by David, when he fled from Saul, in the cave.

Psalms 57

¹ Be merciful to me, God, be merciful to me, For my soul takes refuge in you. Yes, in the shadow of your wings, I will take refuge, Until disaster has passed.

² I cry out to God Most High, To God who accomplishes my requests for me.

³ He will send from heaven, and save me, He rebukes the one who is pursuing me. Selah. God will send out his lovingkindness and his truth.

⁴ My soul is among lions. I lie among those who are set on fire, Even the sons of men, whose teeth are spears and arrows, And their tongue a sharp sword.

⁵ Be exalted, God, above the heavens! Let your glory be above all the earth!

⁶ They have prepared a net for my steps. My soul is bowed down. They dig a pit before me. They fall into the midst of it themselves. Selah.

⁷ My heart is steadfast, God, my heart is steadfast. I will sing, yes, I will sing praises.

⁸ Wake up, my glory! Wake up, psaltery and harp! I will wake up the dawn.

⁹ I will give thanks to you, Lord, among the peoples. I will sing praises to you among the nations.

¹⁰ For your great lovingkindness reaches to the heavens, And your truth to the skies.

¹¹ Be exalted, God, above the heavens. Let your glory be over all the earth. Psalm 58 For the Chief Musician. To the tune of "Do Not Destroy." A poem by David.

Psalms 58

¹ Do you indeed speak righteousness, silent ones? Do you judge blamelessly, you sons of men?
² No, in your heart you plot injustice. You measure out the violence of your hands in the earth.
³ The wicked go astray from the womb. They are wayward as soon as they are born, speaking lies.
⁴ Their poison is like the poison of a snake; Like a deaf cobra that stops its ear,
⁵ Which doesn't listen to the voice of charmers, No matter how skillful the charmer may be.
⁶ Break their teeth, God, in their mouth. Break out the great teeth of the young lions, Yahweh.
⁷ Let them vanish as water that flows away. When they draw the bow, let their arrows be made blunt.
⁸ Let them be as a snail which melts and passes away, Like the stillborn child, who has not seen the sun.
⁹ Before your pots can feel the thorns, He will sweep away, the green and the burning alike.
¹⁰ The righteous shall rejoice when he sees the vengeance. He shall wash his feet in the blood of the wicked;
¹¹ So that men shall say, "Most assuredly there is a reward for the righteous. Most assuredly there is a God who judges the earth." Psalm 59 For the Chief Musician. To the tune of "Do Not Destroy." A poem by David, when Saul sent, and they watched the house to kill him.

Psalms 59

Deliver me from my enemies, my God. Set me on high from those who rise up against me.

2 Deliver me from the workers of iniquity. Save me from the bloodthirsty men.
3 For, behold, they lie in wait for my soul. The mighty gather themselves together against me, Not for my disobedience, nor for my sin, Yahweh.
4 I have done no wrong, yet they are ready to attack me. Rise up, behold, and help me!
5 You, Yahweh God of hosts, the God of Israel, Rouse yourself to punish the nations. Show no mercy to the wicked traitors. Selah.
6 They return at evening, howling like dogs, And prowl around the city.
7 Behold, they spew with their mouth. Swords are in their lips, "For," they say, "who hears us?"
8 But you, Yahweh, laugh at them. You scoff at all the nations.
9 Oh, my Strength, I watch for you, For God is my high tower.
10 My God will go before me with his lovingkindness. God will let me look at my enemies in triumph.
11 Don`t kill them, or my people may forget. Scatter them by your power, and bring them down, Lord our shield.

¹² For the sin of their mouth, and the words of their lips, Let them be caught in their pride, For the curses and lies which they utter.
¹³ Consume them in wrath. Consume them, and they will be no more. Let them know that God rules in Jacob, To the ends of the earth. Selah.
¹⁴ At evening let them return. Let them howl like a dog, and go around the city.
¹⁵ They shall wander up and down for food, And wait all night if they aren`t satisfied.
¹⁶ But I will sing of your strength. Yes, I will sing aloud of your lovingkindness in the morning. For you have been my high tower, A refuge in the day of my distress.
¹⁷ To you, my strength, I will sing praises. For God is my high tower, the God of my mercy. Psalm 60 For the Chief Musician. To the tune of "The Lily of the Covenant." A teaching poem by David, when he fought with Aram-naharaim and with Aram-zobah, and Joab returned, and killed twelve thousand of Edom in the Valley of Salt.

Psalms 60

¹ God, you have rejected us. You have broken us down. You have been angry. Restore us to you, again.
² You have made the land tremble. You have torn it. Mend its fractures, For it quakes.
³ You have shown your people hard things. You have made us drink the wine that makes us stagger.

4 You have given a banner to those who fear you, That it may be displayed because of the truth. Selah.
5 So that your beloved may be delivered, Save with your right hand, and answer us.
6 God has spoken from his sanctuary: "I will triumph. I will divide Shechem, And measure out the valley of Succoth.
7 Gilead is mine, and Manasseh is mine. Ephraim also is the defense of my head. Judah is my scepter.
8 Moab is my wash basin. I will throw my shoe on Edom. I shout in triumph over Philistia."
9 Who will bring me into the strong city? Who has led me to Edom?
10 Haven`t you, God, rejected us? You don`t go out, with our armies, God.
11 Give us help against the adversary, For the help of man is vain.
12 Through God we shall do valiantly, For it is he who will tread down our adversaries. Psalm 61 For the Chief Musician. For a stringed instrument. By David.

Psalms 61

1 Hear my cry, God. Listen to my prayer.
2 From the end of the earth, I will call to you, when my heart is overwhelmed. Lead me to the rock that is higher than I.

3 For you have been a refuge for me, A strong tower from the enemy.
4 I will dwell in your tent forever. I will take refuge in the shelter of your wings. Selah.
5 For you, God, have heard my vows. You have given me the heritage of those who fear your name.
6 You will prolong the king's life; His years shall be for generations.
7 He shall be enthroned in God's presence forever. Appoint your lovingkindness and truth, that they may preserve him.
8 So I will sing praise to your name forever, That I may fulfill my vows daily. Psalm 62 For the Chief Musician. To Jeduthan. A Psalm by David.

Psalms 62

1 My soul rests in God alone. My salvation is from him.
2 He alone is my rock and my salvation, my fortress — I will never be greatly shaken.
3 How long will you assault a man, Would all of you throw him down, Like a leaning wall, like a tottering fence?
4 They fully intend to throw him down from his lofty place. They delight in lies. They bless with their mouth, but they curse inwardly. Selah.
5 My soul, wait in silence for God alone, For my expectation is from him.

⁶ He alone is my rock and my salvation, my fortress. I will not be shaken.
⁷ With God is my salvation and my honor. The rock of my strength, and my refuge, is in God.
⁸ Trust in him at all times, you people. Pour out your heart before him. God is a refuge for us. Selah.
⁹ Surely men of low degree are just a breath, And men of high degree are a lie. In the balances they will go up. They are together lighter than a breath.
¹⁰ Don`t trust in oppression. Don`t become vain in robbery. If riches increase, Don`t set your heart on them.
¹¹ God has spoken once, Twice have I heard this, That power belongs to God.
¹² Also to you, Lord, belongs lovingkindness, For you reward every man according to his work. Psalm 63 A Psalm by David, when he was in the desert of Judah.

Psalms 63

¹ God, you are my God. I will earnestly seek you. My soul thirsts for you, My flesh longs for you, In a dry and weary land, where there is no water.
² So I have seen you in the sanctuary, Watching your power and your glory.
³ Because your lovingkindness is better than life, My lips shall praise you.
⁴ So I will bless you while I live. I will lift up my hands in your name.

⁵ My soul shall be satisfied as with the richest food. My mouth shall praise you with joyful lips,
⁶ When I remember you on my bed, And think about you in the night watches.
⁷ For you have been my help. I will rejoice in the shadow of your wings.
⁸ My soul stays close to you. Your right hand holds me up.
⁹ But those who seek my soul, to destroy it, Shall go into the lower parts of the earth.
¹⁰ They shall be given over to the power of the sword. They shall be jackal food.
¹¹ But the king shall rejoice in God. Everyone who swears by him will praise him, For the mouth of those who speak lies shall be silenced. Psalm 64 For the Chief Musician. A Psalm by David.

Psalms 64

¹ Hear my voice, God, in my complaint. Preserve my life from fear of the enemy.
² Hide me from the conspiracy of the wicked, From the noisy crowd of the ones doing evil;
³ Who sharpen their tongue like a sword, And aim their arrows, deadly words,
⁴ To shoot innocent men from ambushes. They shoot at him suddenly and fearlessly.

⁵ They encourage themselves in evil plans. They talk about laying snares secretly. They say, "Who will see them?"
⁶ They plot injustice, saying, "We have made a perfect plan!" Surely man`s mind and heart are cunning.
⁷ But God will shoot at them. They will be suddenly struck down with an arrow.
⁸ Their own tongues shall ruin them. All who see them will shake their heads.
⁹ All mankind shall be afraid. They shall declare the work of God, And shall wisely ponder what he has done.
¹⁰ The righteous shall be glad in Yahweh, And shall take refuge in him. All the upright in heart shall praise him! Psalm 65 For the Chief Musician. A Psalm by David. A song.

Psalms 65

¹ Praise waits for you, God, in Zion. To you shall vows be performed.
² You who hear prayer, To you all men will come.
³ Sins overwhelmed me, But you atoned for our transgressions.
⁴ Blessed is one whom you choose, and cause to come near, That he may live in your courts. We will be filled with the goodness of your house, Your holy temple.

⁵ By awesome deeds of righteousness, you answer us, God of our salvation. You who are the hope of all the ends of the earth, Of those who are far away on the sea;
⁶ Who by his power forms the mountains, Having armed yourself with strength;
⁷ Who stills the roaring of the seas, The roaring of their waves, And the turmoil of the nations.
⁸ They also who dwell in far-away places are afraid at your wonders. You call the morning`s dawn and the evening with songs of joy.
⁹ You visit the earth, and water it. You greatly enrich it. The river of God is full of water. You provide them grain, for so you have ordained it.
¹⁰ You drench its furrows. You level its ridges. You soften it with showers. You bless it with a crop.
¹¹ You crown the year with your bounty. Your carts overflow with abundance.
¹² The wilderness grasslands overflow. The hills are clothed with gladness.
¹³ The pastures are covered with flocks. The valleys also are clothed with grain. They shout for joy! They also sing. Psalm 66 For the Chief Musician. A song. A Psalm.

Psalms 66

¹ Make a joyful noise to God, all the earth!
² Sing to the glory of his name! Offer glory and praise!

³ Tell God, "How awesome are your deeds! Through the greatness of your power, Your enemies will submit themselves to you.
⁴ All the earth will worship you, And will sing to you; They will sing to your name." Selah.
⁵ Come, and see God's deeds — Awesome work on behalf of the children of men.
⁶ He turned the sea into dry land. They went through the river on foot. There, we rejoiced in him.
⁷ He rules by his might forever. His eyes watch the nations. Don't let the rebellious rise up against him. Selah.
⁸ Praise our God, you peoples! Make the sound of his praise heard,
⁹ Who preserves our life among the living, And doesn't allow our feet to be moved.
¹⁰ For you, God, have tested us. You have refined us, as silver is refined.
¹¹ You brought us into prison. You laid a burden on our backs.
¹² You allowed men to ride over our heads. We went through fire and through water, But you brought us to the place of abundance.
¹³ I will come into your temple with burnt offerings. I will pay my vows to you,
¹⁴ which my lips promised, And my mouth spoke, when I was in distress.
¹⁵ I will offer to you burnt offerings of fat animals, With the offering of rams, I will offer bulls with goats. Selah.

[16] Come, and hear, all you who fear God. I will declare what he has done for my soul.
[17] I cried to him with my mouth. He was extolled with my tongue.
[18] If I cherished sin in my heart, The Lord wouldn't have listened.
[19] But most assuredly, God has listened. He has heard the voice of my prayer.
[20] Blessed be God, who has not turned away my prayer, Nor his lovingkindness from me. Psalm 67 For the Chief Musician. With stringed instruments. A Psalm. A song.

Psalms 67

[1] May God be merciful to us, bless us, And cause his face to shine on us. Selah.
[2] That your way may be known on earth, And your salvation among all nations,
[3] Let the peoples praise you, God. Let all the peoples praise you.
[4] Oh let the nations be glad and sing for joy, For you will judge the peoples with equity, And govern the nations on earth. Selah.
[5] Let the peoples praise you, God. Let all the peoples praise you.
[6] The earth has yielded its increase. God, even our own God, will bless us.

⁷ God will bless us. All the ends of the earth shall fear him. Psalm 68 For the Chief Musician. A Psalm by David. A song.

Psalms 68

¹ Let God arise! Let his enemies be scattered! Let them who hate him also flee before him.
² As smoke is driven away, so drive them away. As wax melts before the fire, So let the wicked perish at the presence of God.
³ But let the righteous be glad. Let them rejoice before God. Yes, let them rejoice with gladness.
⁴ Sing to God! Sing praises to his name! Extol him who rides on the clouds — To Yah, his name! Rejoice before him.
⁵ A father of the fatherless, and a defender of the widows, Is God in his holy habitation.
⁶ God sets the lonely in families. He brings out the prisoners with singing, But the rebellious dwell in a sun-scorched land.
⁷ God, when you went forth before your people, When you marched through the wilderness… Selah.
⁸ The earth trembled. The sky also poured down rain at the presence of the God of Sinai — At the presence of God, the God of Israel.
⁹ You, God, sent a plentiful rain. You confirmed your inheritance, when it was weary.

¹⁰ Your congregation lived therein. You, God, prepared your goodness for the poor.
¹¹ The Lord announced the word. The ones who proclaim it are a great company.
¹² "Kings of armies flee! They flee!" She who waits at home divides the spoil,
¹³ While you sleep among the campfires, The wings of a dove sheathed with silver, Her feathers with shining gold.
¹⁴ When the Almighty scattered kings in her, It snowed on Zalmon.
¹⁵ The mountains of Bashan are majestic mountains. The mountains of Bashan are rugged.
¹⁶ Why do you look in envy, you rugged mountains, At the mountain where God chooses to reign? Yes, Yahweh will dwell there forever.
¹⁷ The chariots of God are tens of thousands and thousands of thousands. The Lord is among them, from Sinai, into the sanctuary.
¹⁸ You have ascended on high. You have led away captives. You have received gifts among men, Yes, among the rebellious also, that Yah God might dwell there.
¹⁹ Blessed be the Lord, who daily bears our burdens, Even the God who is our salvation. Selah.
²⁰ God is to us a God of deliverance. To Yahweh, the Lord, belongs escape from death.
²¹ But God will strike through the head of his enemies, The hairy scalp of such a one as still continues in his guiltiness.

²² The Lord said, "I will bring you again from Bashan, I will bring you again from the depths of the sea;
²³ That you may crush them, dipping your foot in blood, That the tongues of your dogs may have their portion from your enemies."
²⁴ They have seen your goings, God, Even the goings of my God, my King, into the sanctuary.
²⁵ The singers went before, the minstrels followed after, In the midst of the ladies playing with tambourines,
²⁶ "Bless God in the congregations, Even the Lord in the assembly of Israel!"
²⁷ There is little Benjamin, their ruler, The princes of Judah, their council, The princes of Zebulun, and the princes of Naphtali.
²⁸ Your God has commanded your strength. Strengthen, God, that which you have done for us.
²⁹ Because of your temple at Jerusalem, Kings shall bring presents to you.
³⁰ Rebuke the wild animal of the reeds, The multitude of the bulls, with the calves of the peoples. Being humbled, may it bring bars of silver. Scatter the nations that delight in war.
³¹ Princes shall come out of Egypt. Ethiopia shall hurry to stretch out her hands to God.
³² Sing to God, you kingdoms of the earth! Sing praises to the Lord! Selah.
³³ To him who rides on the heaven of heavens, which are of old; Behold, he utters his voice, a mighty voice.
³⁴ Ascribe strength to God! His excellency is over Israel, His strength is in the skies.

35 You are awesome, God, in your sanctuaries. The God of Israel gives strength and power to his people. Praise be to God! Psalm 69 For the Chief Musician. To the tune of "Lilies." By David.

Psalms 69

1 Save me, God, For the waters have come up to my neck!
2 I sink in deep mire, where there is no foothold. I have come into deep waters, where the floods overflow me.
3 I am weary with my crying. My throat is dry. My eyes fail, looking for my God.
4 Those who hate me without a cause are more than the hairs of my head. Those who want to cut me off, being my enemies wrongfully, are mighty. I have to restore what I didn't take away.
5 God, you know my foolishness. My sins aren't hidden from you.
6 Don't let those who wait for you be put to shame through me, Lord Yahweh of Hosts. Don't let those who seek you be brought to dishonor through me, God of Israel.
7 Because for your sake, I have borne reproach. Shame has covered my face.
8 I have become a stranger to my brothers, An alien to my mother's children.

9 For the zeal of your house consumes me. The reproaches of those who reproach you have fallen on me.
10 When I wept and I fasted, That was to my reproach.
11 When I made sackcloth my clothing, I became a byword to them.
12 Those who sit in the gate talk about me. I am the song of the drunkards.
13 But as for me, my prayer is to you, Yahweh, in an acceptable time. God, in the abundance of your lovingkindness, answer me in the truth of your salvation.
14 Deliver me out of the mire, and don't let me sink. Let me be delivered from those who hate me, and out of the deep waters.
15 Don't let the flood waters overwhelm me, Neither let the deep swallow me up. Don't let the pit shut its mouth on me.
16 Answer me, Yahweh, for your lovingkindness is good. According to the multitude of your tender mercies, turn to me.
17 Don't hide your face from your servant, For I am in distress. Answer me speedily!
18 Draw near to my soul, and redeem it. Ransom me because of my enemies.
19 You know my reproach, my shame, and my dishonor. My adversaries are all before you.
20 Reproach has broken my heart, and I am full of heaviness. I looked for some to take pity, but there was none; For comforters, but I found none.
21 They also gave me gall for my food. In my thirst, they gave me vinegar to drink.

²² Let their table before them become a snare. May it become a retribution and a trap.
²³ Let their eyes be darkened, so that they can't see. Make their loins continually to shake.
²⁴ Pour out your indignation on them. Let the fierceness of your anger overtake them.
²⁵ Let their habitation be desolate. Let no one dwell in their tents.
²⁶ For they persecute him whom you have wounded. They tell of the sorrow of those whom you have hurt.
²⁷ Charge them with crime upon crime. Don't let them come into your righteousness.
²⁸ Let them be blotted out of the book of life, And not be written with the righteous.
²⁹ But I am in pain and distress. Let your salvation, God, protect me.
³⁰ I will praise the name of God with a song, And will magnify him with thanksgiving.
³¹ It will please Yahweh better than an ox, Or a bull that has horns and hoofs.
³² The humble have seen it, and are glad. You who seek after God, let your heart live.
³³ For Yahweh hears the needy, And doesn't despise his captive people.
³⁴ Let heaven and earth praise him; The seas, and everything that moves therein!
³⁵ For God will save Zion, and build the cities of Judah. They shall settle there, and own it.

³⁶ The children also of his servants shall inherit it. Those who love his name shall dwell therein. Psalm 70 For the Chief Musician. By David. A reminder.

Psalms 70

¹ Hurry, God, to deliver me. Come quickly to help me, Yahweh.
² Let them be put to shame and confounded who seek my soul. Let those who desire my ruin be turned back in disgrace.
³ Let them be turned because of their shame Who say, "Aha! Aha!"
⁴ Let all those who seek you rejoice and be glad in you. Let those who love your salvation continually say, "Let God be exalted!"
⁵ But I am poor and needy. Come to me quickly, God. You are my help and my deliverer, Yahweh, don`t delay. Psalm 71

Psalms 71

¹ In you, Yahweh, I take refuge. Never let me be put to shame.
² Deliver me in your righteousness, and rescue me. Turn your ear to me, and save me.

³ Be to me a rock of refuge to which I may always go. Give the command to save me, For you are my rock and my fortress.
⁴ Rescue me, my God, from the hand of the wicked, From the hand of the unrighteous and cruel man.
⁵ For you are my hope, Lord Yahweh; My confidence from my youth.
⁶ I have relied on you from the womb. You are he who took me out of my mother's womb. I will always praise you.
⁷ I am a marvel to many, But you are my strong refuge.
⁸ My mouth shall be filled with your praise, With your honor all the day.
⁹ Don't reject me in my old age. Don't forsake me when my strength fails.
¹⁰ For my enemies talk about me. Those who watch for my soul conspire together,
¹¹ Saying, "God has forsaken him. Pursue and take him, for no one will rescue him."
¹² God, don't be far from me. My God, hurry to help me.
¹³ Let my accusers be put to shame and consumed. Let them be covered with disgrace and scorn who want to harm me.
¹⁴ But I will always hope, And will add to all of your praise.
¹⁵ My mouth will tell about your righteousness, And of your salvation all day, Though I don't know its full measure.

16 I will come with the mighty acts of the Lord Yahweh. I will make mention of your righteousness, even of yours alone.
17 God, you have taught me from my youth. Until now, I have declared your wondrous works.
18 Yes, even when I am old and gray-headed, God, don't forsake me, Until I have declared your strength to the next generation, Your might to everyone who is to come.
19 Your righteousness also, God, reaches to the heavens; You who have done great things. God, who is like you?
20 You, who have showed us many and bitter troubles, You will let me live. You will bring us up again from the depths of the earth.
21 Increase my honor, And comfort me again.
22 I will also praise you with the harp for your faithfulness, my God. I sing praises to you with the lyre, Holy One of Israel.
23 My lips shall shout for joy! My soul, which you have redeemed, sings praises to you!
24 My tongue will also talk about your righteousness all day long, For they are put to shame, and they are confounded, who want to harm me. Psalm 72 By Solomon.

Psalms 72

1 God, give the king your justice; Your righteousness to the royal son.
2 He will judge your people with righteousness, And your poor with justice.

³ The mountains shall bring prosperity to the people; The hills bring the fruit of righteousness.
⁴ He will judge the poor of the people. He will save the children of the needy, And will break the oppressor in pieces.
⁵ They shall fear you while the sun endures; And as long as the moon, throughout all generations.
⁶ He will come down like rain on the mown grass, As showers that water the earth.
⁷ In his days, the righteous shall flourish, And abundance of peace, until the moon is no more.
⁸ He shall have dominion also from sea to sea, From the River to the ends of the earth.
⁹ Those who dwell in the wilderness shall bow before him. His enemies shall lick the dust.
¹⁰ The kings of Tarshish and of the isles will bring tribute. The kings of Sheba and Seba shall offer gifts.
¹¹ Yes, all kings shall fall down before him. All nations shall serve him.
¹² For he will deliver the needy when he cries; The poor, who has no helper.
¹³ He will have pity on the poor and needy. He will save the souls of the needy.
¹⁴ He will redeem their soul from oppression and violence. Their blood will be precious in his sight.
¹⁵ They shall live, and to him shall be given of the gold of Sheba. Men shall pray for him continually. They shall bless him all day long.

[16] There shall be abundance of grain throughout the land. Its fruit sways like Lebanon. Let it flourish, thriving like the grass of the field.

[17] His name endures forever. His name continues as long as the sun. Men shall be blessed by him. All nations will call him blessed.

[18] Praise be to Yahweh God, the God of Israel, Who alone does marvelous deeds.

[19] Blessed be his glorious name forever! Let the whole earth be filled with his glory! Amen and amen.

[20] This ends the prayers by David, the son of Jesse.
BOOK III Psalm 73 A Psalm by Asaph.

Psalms 73

[1] Surely God is good to Israel, To those who are pure in heart.

[2] But as for me, my feet were almost gone. My steps had nearly slipped.

[3] For I was envious of the arrogant, When I saw the prosperity of the wicked.

[4] For there are no struggles in their death, But their strength is firm.

[5] They are free from burdens of men, Neither are they plagued like other men.

[6] Therefore pride is like a chain around their neck. Violence covers them like a garment.

7 Their eyes bulge with fat. Their minds pass the limits of conceit.
8 They scoff and speak with malice. In arrogance, they threaten oppression.
9 They have set their mouth in the heavens. Their tongue walks through the earth.
10 Therefore their people return to them, And they drink up waters of abundance.
11 They say, "How does God know? Is there knowledge in the Most High?"
12 Behold, these are the wicked. Being always at ease, they increase in riches.
13 Surely in vain I have cleansed my heart, And washed my hands in innocence,
14 For all day long have I been plagued, And punished every morning.
15 If I had said, "I will speak thus;" Behold, I would have betrayed the generation of your children.
16 When I tried to understand this, It was too painful for me;
17 Until I entered God`s sanctuary, And considered their latter end.
18 Surely you set them in slippery places. You throw them down to destruction.
19 How they are suddenly destroyed! They are completely swept away with terrors.
20 As a dream when one wakes up, So, Lord, when you awake, you will despise their fantasies.
21 For my soul was grieved. I was embittered in my heart.

22 I was so senseless and ignorant. I was a brute beast before you.
23 Nevertheless, I am continually with you. You have held my right hand.
24 You will guide me with your counsel, And afterward receive me to glory.
25 Who do I have in heaven? There is no one on earth who I desire besides you.
26 My flesh and my heart fails, But God is the strength of my heart and my portion forever.
27 For, behold, those who are far from you shall perish. You have destroyed all those who are unfaithful to you.
28 But it is good for me to come close to God. I have made the Lord Yahweh my refuge, That I may tell of all your works. Psalm 74 A contemplation by Asaph.

Psalms 74

1 God, why have you rejected us forever? Why does your anger smolder against the sheep of your pasture?
2 Remember your congregation, which you purchased of old, Which you have redeemed to be the tribe of your inheritance; Mount Zion, in which you have lived.
3 Lift up your feet to the perpetual ruins, All the evil that the enemy has done in the sanctuary.
4 Your adversaries have roared in the midst of your assembly. They have set up their standards as signs.

⁵ They behaved like men wielding axes, Cutting through a thicket of trees.
⁶ Now all its carved work They break down with hatchet and hammers.
⁷ They have burned your sanctuary to the ground. They have profaned the dwelling-place of your Name.
⁸ They said in their heart, "We will crush them completely." They have burned up all the places in the land where God was worshipped.
⁹ We see no miraculous signs. There is no longer any prophet, Neither is there among us anyone who knows how long.
¹⁰ How long, God, shall the adversary reproach? Shall the enemy blaspheme your name forever?
¹¹ Why do you draw back your hand, even your right hand? Take it out of your pocket and consume them!
¹² Yet God is my King of old, Working salvation in the midst of the earth.
¹³ You divided the sea by your strength. You broke the heads of the sea monsters in the waters.
¹⁴ You broke the heads of Leviathan in pieces. You gave him as food to people and desert creatures.
¹⁵ You opened up spring and stream. You dried up mighty rivers.
¹⁶ The day is yours, the night is also yours. You have prepared the light and the sun.
¹⁷ You have set all the boundaries of the earth. You have made summer and winter.
¹⁸ Remember this, that the enemy has mocked you, Yahweh. Foolish people have blasphemed your name.

¹⁹ Don`t deliver the soul of your dove to wild beasts. Don`t forget the life of your poor forever.
²⁰ Honor your covenant, For haunts of violence fill the dark places of the earth.
²¹ Don`t let the oppressed return ashamed. Let the poor and needy praise your name.
²² Arise, God! Plead your own cause. Remember how the foolish man mocks you all day.
²³ Don`t forget the voice of your adversaries. The tumult of those who rise up against you ascends continually.
Psalm 75 For the Chief Musician. To the tune of "Do Not Destroy." A Psalm by Asaph. A song.

Psalms 75

¹ We give thanks to you, God, We give thanks, for your Name is near. Men tell about your wondrous works.
² When I choose the appointed time, I will judge blamelessly.
³ The earth and all its inhabitants quake. I firmly hold its pillars. Selah.
⁴ I said to the arrogant, "Don`t boast;" To the wicked, "Don`t lift up the horn.
⁵ Don`t lift up your horn on high. Don`t speak with a stiff neck."
⁶ For neither from the east, nor from the west, Nor yet from the south, comes exaltation.

⁷ But God is the judge. He puts down one, and lifts up another.
⁸ For in the hand of Yahweh there is a cup, Full of foaming wine mixed with spices. He pours it out. Indeed the wicked of the earth drink and drink it to its very dregs.
⁹ But I will declare this forever: I will sing praises to the God of Jacob.
¹⁰ I will cut off all the horns of the wicked, But the horns of the righteous shall be lifted up. Psalm 76 For the Chief Musician. On stringed instruments. A Psalm by Asaph. A song.

Psalms 76

¹ In Judah, God is known. His name is great in Israel.
² His tent is also in Salem; His dwelling-place in Zion.
³ There he broke the flaming arrows of the bow, The shield, and the sword, and the weapons of war. Selah.
⁴ Glorious are you, and excellent, More than mountains of game.
⁵ Valiant men lie plundered, They have slept their last sleep. None of the men of war can lift their hands.
⁶ At your rebuke, God of Jacob, Both chariot and horse are cast into a deep sleep.
⁷ You, even you, are to be feared. Who can stand in your sight when you are angry?

⁸ You pronounced judgment from heaven. The earth feared, and was silent,
⁹ When God arose to judgment, To save all the afflicted ones of the earth. Selah.
¹⁰ Surely the wrath of man praises you. The survivors of your wrath are restrained.
¹¹ Make vows to Yahweh your God, and fulfill them! Let all of his neighbors bring presents to him who is to be feared.
¹² He will cut off the spirit of princes. He is feared by the kings of the earth. Psalm 77 For the Chief Musician. To Jeduthun. A Psalm by Asaph.

Psalms 77

¹ My cry goes to God! Indeed, I cry to God for help, And for him to listen to me.
² In the day of my trouble I sought the Lord. My hand was stretched out in the night, and didn't get tired. My soul refused to be comforted.
³ I remember God, and I groan. I complain, and my spirit is overwhelmed. Selah.
⁴ You hold my eyelids open. I am so troubled that I can't speak.
⁵ I have considered the days of old, The years of ancient times.
⁶ I remember my song in the night. I consider in my own heart; My spirit diligently inquires:

7 "Will the Lord reject us forever? Will he be favorable no more?
8 Has his lovingkindness vanished forever? Does his promise fail for generations?
9 Has God forgotten to be gracious? Has he, in anger, withheld his compassion?" Selah.
10 Then I thought, "I will appeal to this: The years of the right hand of the Most High."
11 I will remember Yah`s deeds; For I will remember your wonders of old.
12 I will also meditate on all your work, And consider your doings.
13 Your way, God, is in the sanctuary. What god is great like God?
14 You are the God who does wonders. You have made your strength known among the peoples.
15 You have redeemed your people with your arm, The sons of Jacob and Joseph. Selah.
16 The waters saw you, God. The waters saw you, and they writhed. The depths also convulsed.
17 The clouds poured out water. The skies resounded with thunder. Your arrows also flashed around.
18 The voice of your thunder was in the whirlwind. The lightnings lit up the world. The earth trembled and shook.
19 Your way was through the sea; Your paths through the great waters. Your footsteps were not known.
20 You led your people like a flock, By the hand of Moses and Aaron. Psalm 78 A contemplation by Asaph.

Psalms 78

1 Hear my law, my people. Turn your ears to the words of my mouth.
2 I will open my mouth in a parable. I will utter dark sayings of old,
3 Which we have heard and known, Our fathers have told us.
4 We will not hide them from their children, Telling to the generation to come the praises of Yahweh, His strength, and his wondrous works that he has done.
5 For he established a testimony in Jacob, And appointed a law in Israel, Which he commanded our fathers, That they should make them known to their children;
6 That the generation to come might know, even the children who should be born; Who should arise and tell their children,
7 That they might set their hope in God, And not forget the works of God, But keep his commandments,
8 And might not be as their fathers, A stubborn and rebellious generation, A generation that didn`t make their hearts loyal, Whose spirit was not steadfast with God.
9 The children of Ephraim, being armed and carrying bows, Turned back in the day of battle.
10 They didn`t keep the covenant of God, And refused to walk in his law.
11 They forgot his doings, His wondrous works that he had showed them.

12 Marvelous things did he in the sight of their fathers, In the land of Egypt, in the field of Zoan.
13 He split the sea, and caused them to pass through; He made the waters stand as a heap.
14 In the daytime he also led them with a cloud, All the night with a light of fire.
15 He split rocks in the wilderness, And gave them drink abundantly as out of the depths.
16 He brought streams also out of the rock, And caused waters to run down like rivers.
17 Yet they still went on to sin against him, To rebel against the Most High in the desert.
18 They tempted God in their heart By asking food according to their desire.
19 Yes, they spoke against God. They said, "Can God prepare a table in the wilderness?
20 Behold, he struck the rock, so that waters gushed out, Streams overflowed. Can he give bread also? Will he provide flesh for his people?"
21 Therefore Yahweh heard, and was angry. A fire was kindled against Jacob, Anger also went up against Israel,
22 Because they didn`t believe in God, And didn`t trust in his salvation.
23 Yet he commanded the skies above, And opened the doors of heaven.
24 He rained down manna on them to eat, And gave them food from the sky.
25 Man ate the bread of angels. He sent them food to the full.

26 He caused the east wind to blow in the sky. By his power he guided the south wind.
27 He rained also flesh on them as the dust; Winged birds as the sand of the seas.
28 He let them fall in the midst of their camp, Around their habitations.
29 So they ate, and were well filled. He gave them their own desire.
30 They didn't turn from their cravings. Their food was yet in their mouths,
31 When the anger of God went up against them, And killed some of the fattest of them, And struck down the young men of Israel.
32 For all this they still sinned, And didn't believe in his wondrous works.
33 Therefore he consumed their days in vanity, And their years in terror.
34 When he killed them, then they inquired after him. They returned and sought God earnestly.
35 They remembered that God was their rock, The Most High God their redeemer.
36 But they flattered him with their mouth, And lied to him with their tongue.
37 For their heart was not right with him, Neither were they faithful in his covenant.
38 But he, being merciful, forgave iniquity, and didn't destroy them. Yes, many times he turned his anger away, And didn't stir up all his wrath.
39 He remembered that they were but flesh, A wind that passes away, and doesn't come again.

⁴⁰ How often did they rebel against him in the wilderness, And grieve him in the desert!
⁴¹ They turned again and tempted God, And provoked the Holy One of Israel.
⁴² They didn't remember his hand, Nor the day when he redeemed them from the adversary;
⁴³ How he set his signs in Egypt, His wonders in the field of Zoan,
⁴⁴ Turned their rivers into blood, Their streams, so that they could not drink.
⁴⁵ He sent among them swarms of flies, which devoured them; Frogs, which destroyed them.
⁴⁶ He gave also their increase to the caterpillar, Their labor to the locust.
⁴⁷ He destroyed their vines with hail, Their sycamore-fig trees with frost.
⁴⁸ He gave over their cattle also to the hail, And their flocks to hot thunderbolts.
⁴⁹ He threw on them the fierceness of his anger, Wrath, indignation, and trouble, And a band of angels of evil.
⁵⁰ He made a path for his anger. He didn't spare their soul from death, But gave their life over to the pestilence,
⁵¹ And struck all the firstborn in Egypt, The chief of their strength in the tents of Ham.
⁵² But he led forth his own people like sheep, And guided them in the wilderness like a flock.
⁵³ He led them safely, so that they weren't afraid, But the sea overwhelmed their enemies.
⁵⁴ He brought them to the border of his sanctuary, To this mountain, which his right hand had taken.

⁵⁵ He also drove out the nations before them, Allotted them for an inheritance by line, And made the tribes of Israel to dwell in their tents.
⁵⁶ Yet they tempted and rebelled against the Most High God, And didn't keep his testimonies;
⁵⁷ But turned back, and dealt treacherously like their fathers. They were turned aside like a deceitful bow.
⁵⁸ For they provoked him to anger with their high places, And moved him to jealousy with their engraved images.
⁵⁹ When God heard this, he was angry, And greatly abhorred Israel;
⁶⁰ So that he forsook the tent of Shiloh, The tent which he placed among men;
⁶¹ And delivered his strength into captivity, His glory into the adversary's hand.
⁶² He also gave his people over to the sword, And was angry with his inheritance.
⁶³ Fire devoured their young men; Their virgins had no wedding song.
⁶⁴ Their priests fell by the sword; Their widows made no lamentation.
⁶⁵ Then the Lord awakened as one out of sleep, Like a mighty man who shouts by reason of wine.
⁶⁶ He struck his adversaries backward. He put them to a perpetual reproach.
⁶⁷ Moreover he rejected the tent of Joseph, And didn't choose the tribe of Ephraim,
⁶⁸ But chose the tribe of Judah, Mount Zion which he loved.

⁶⁹ He built his sanctuary like the heights, Like the earth which he has established forever.
⁷⁰ He also chose David his servant, And took him from the sheepfolds;
⁷¹ From following the ewes that have their young he brought him To be the shepherd of Jacob, his people, and Israel, his inheritance.
⁷² So he was their shepherd according to the integrity of his heart, And guided them by the skillfulness of his hands. Psalm 79 A Psalm by Asaph.

Psalms 79

¹ God, the nations have come into your inheritance. They have defiled your holy temple. They have laid Jerusalem in heaps.
² They have given the dead bodies of your servants to be food for the birds of the sky, The flesh of your saints to the animals of the earth.
³ Their blood they have shed like water around Jerusalem. There was no one to bury them.
⁴ We have become a reproach to our neighbors, A scoffing and derision to those who are around us.
⁵ How long, Yahweh? Will you be angry forever? Will your jealousy burn like fire?
⁶ Pour out your wrath on the nations that don`t know you; On the kingdoms that don`t call on your names;

⁷ For they have devoured Jacob, And destroyed his homeland.
⁸ Don't hold the iniquities of our forefathers against us. Let your tender mercies speedily meet us, For we are in desperate need.
⁹ Help us, God of our salvation, for the glory of your name. Deliver us, and forgive our sins, for your name's sake.
¹⁰ Why should the nations say, "Where is their God?" Let it be known among the nations, before our eyes, That vengeance for your servants' blood is being poured out.
¹¹ Let the sighing of the prisoner come before you. According to the greatness of your power, preserve those who are sentenced to death;
¹² Pay back to our neighbors seven times into their bosom Their reproach with which they have reproached you, Lord.
¹³ So we, your people and sheep of your pasture, Will give you thanks forever. We will praise you forever, to all generations. Psalm 80 For the Chief Musician. To the tune of "The Lilies of the Covenant." A Psalm by Asaph.

Psalms 80

¹ Hear us, Shepherd of Israel, You who lead Joseph like a flock, You who sit above the cherubim, shine forth.
² Before Ephraim and Benjamin and Manasseh, stir up your might, Come to save us.

³ Turn us again, God. Cause your face to shine, And we will be saved.
⁴ Yahweh God of hosts, How long will you be angry against the prayer of your people?
⁵ You have fed them with the bread of tears, And given them tears to drink in large measure.
⁶ You make us a source of contention to our neighbors. Our enemies laugh among themselves.
⁷ Turn us again, God of hosts. Cause your face to shine, And we will be saved.
⁸ You brought a vine out of Egypt. You drove out the nations, and planted it.
⁹ You cleared the ground for it. It took deep root, and filled the land.
¹⁰ The mountains were covered with its shadow. Its boughs were like God's cedars.
¹¹ It sent out its branches to the sea, Its shoots to the River.
¹² Why have you broken down its walls, So that all those who pass by the way pluck it?
¹³ The boar out of the wood ravages it. The wild animals of the field feed on it.
¹⁴ Turn again, we beg you, God of hosts. Look down from heaven, and see, and visit this vine,
¹⁵ The stock which your right hand planted, The branch that you made strong for yourself.
¹⁶ It is burned with fire. It is cut down. They perish at your rebuke.
¹⁷ Let your hand be on the man of your right hand, On the son of man whom you made strong for yourself.

¹⁸ So we will not turn away from you. Revive us, and we will call on your name.
¹⁹ Turn us again, Yahweh God of hosts. Cause your face to shine, and we will be saved. Psalm 81 For the Chief Musician. On an instrument of Gath. By Asaph.

Psalms 81

¹ Sing aloud to God, our strength! Make a joyful noise to the God of Jacob!
² Raise a song, and bring here the tambourine, The pleasant lyre with the harp.
³ Blow the trumpet at the New Moon, At the full moon, on our feast day.
⁴ For it is a statute for Israel, An ordinance of the God of Jacob.
⁵ He appointed it in Joseph for a testimony, When he went out over the land of Egypt, I heard a language that I didn`t know.
⁶ "I removed his shoulder from the burden. His hands were freed from the basket.
⁷ You called in trouble, and I delivered you. I answered you in the secret place of thunder. I tested you at the waters of Meribah." Selah.
⁸ "Hear, my people, and I will testify to you. Israel, if you would listen to me!
⁹ There shall be no strange god in you, Neither shall you worship any foreign god.

10 I am Yahweh, your God, Who brought you up out of the land of Egypt. Open your mouth wide, and I will fill it.
11 But my people didn`t listen to my voice. Israel desired none of me.
12 So I let them go after the stubbornness of their hearts, That they might walk in their own counsels.
13 Oh that my people would listen to me, That Israel would walk in my ways!
14 I would soon subdue their enemies, And turn my hand against their adversaries.
15 The haters of Yahweh would cringe before him, And their punishment would last forever.
16 But he would have also fed them with the finest of the wheat. I will satisfy you with honey out of the rock."
Psalm 82 A Psalm by Asaph.

Psalms 82

1 God presides in the great assembly. He judges among the gods.
2 "How long will you judge unjustly, And show partiality to the wicked?" Selah.
3 "Defend the weak, the poor, and the fatherless. Maintain the rights of the poor and oppressed.
4 Rescue the weak and needy. Deliver them out of the hand of the wicked."

⁵ They don`t know, neither do they understand. They walk back and forth in darkness. All the foundations of the earth are shaken.
⁶ I said, "You are gods, All of you are sons of the Most High.
⁷ Nevertheless you shall die like men, And fall like one of the rulers."
⁸ Arise, God, judge the earth, For you inherit all of the nations. Psalm 83 A song. A Psalm by Asaph.

Psalms 83

¹ God, don`t keep silent. Don`t keep silent, and don`t be still, God.
² For, behold, your enemies are stirred up. Those who hate you have lifted up their heads.
³ They conspire with cunning against your people. They plot against your cherished ones.
⁴ "Come," they say, "and let us destroy them as a nation, That the name of Israel may be remembered no more."
⁵ For they have conspired together with one mind. They form an alliance against you.
⁶ The tents of Edom and the Ishmaelites; Moab, and the Hagrites;
⁷ Gebal, Ammon, and Amalek; Philistia with the inhabitants of Tyre;
⁸ Assyria also is joined with them. They have helped the children of Lot. Selah.

9 Do to them as you did to Midian, As to Sisera, as to Jabin, at the river Kishon;

10 Who perished at Endor, Who became as dung for the earth.

11 Make their nobles like Oreb and Zeeb; Yes, all their princes like Zebah and Zalmunna;

12 Who said, "Let us take possession Of God`s pasturelands."

13 My God, make them like tumbleweed; Like chaff before the wind.

14 As the fire that burns the forest, As the flame that sets the mountains on fire,

15 So pursue them with your tempest, Terrify them with your storm.

16 Fill their faces with confusion, That they may seek your name, Yahweh.

17 Let them be put to shame and dismayed forever. Yes, let them be confounded and perish;

18 That they may know that you alone, whose name is Yahweh, Are the Most High over all the earth. Psalm 84 For the Chief Musician. On an instrument of Gath. A Psalm by the sons of Korah.

Psalms 84

1 How lovely are your dwellings, Yahweh of Hosts!

² My soul longs, and even faints for the courts of Yahweh. My heart and my flesh cry out for the living God.
³ Yes, the sparrow has found a home, And the swallow a nest for herself, where she may have her young, Near your altars, Yahweh of Hosts, My King, and my God.
⁴ Blessed are those who dwell in your house. They are always praising you. Selah.
⁵ Blessed is the man whose strength is in you; Who have set their hearts on a pilgrimage.
⁶ Passing through the valley of Weeping, they make it a place of springs. Yes, the autumn rain covers it with blessings.
⁷ They go from strength to strength. Everyone of them appears before God in Zion.
⁸ Yahweh, God of hosts, hear my prayer. Listen, God of Jacob. Selah.
⁹ Behold, God our shield, Look at the face of your anointed.
¹⁰ For a day in your courts is better than a thousand. I would rather be a doorkeeper in the house of my God, Than to dwell in the tents of wickedness.
¹¹ For Yahweh God is a sun and a shield. Yahweh will give grace and glory. He withholds no good thing from those who walk blamelessly.
¹² Yahweh of Hosts, Blessed is the man who trusts in you. Psalm 85 For the Chief Musician. A Psalm by the sons of Korah.

Psalms 85

¹ Yahweh, you have been favorable to your land. You have restored the fortunes of Jacob.
² You have forgiven the iniquity of your people. You have covered all their sin. Selah.
³ You have taken away all your wrath. You have turned from the fierceness of your anger.
⁴ Turn us, God of our salvation, And cause your indignation toward us to cease.
⁵ Will you be angry with us forever? Will you draw out your anger to all generations?
⁶ Won't you revive us again, That your people may rejoice in you?
⁷ Show us your lovingkindness, Yahweh. Grant us your salvation.
⁸ I will hear what God, Yahweh, will speak, For he will speak peace to his people, his saints; But let them not turn again to folly.
⁹ Surely his salvation is near those who fear him, That glory may dwell in our land.
¹⁰ Mercy and truth meet together. Righteousness and peace have kissed each other.
¹¹ Truth springs out of the earth. Righteousness has looked down from heaven.
¹² Yes, Yahweh will give that which is good. Our land will yield its increase.
¹³ Righteousness goes before him, And prepares the way for his steps. Psalm 86 A Prayer by David.

Psalms 86

¹ Hear, Yahweh, and answer me, For I am poor and needy.
² Preserve my soul, for I am godly. You, my God, save your servant who trusts in you.
³ Be merciful to me, Lord, For I call to you all day long.
⁴ Bring joy to the soul of your servant, For to you, Lord, do I lift up my soul.
⁵ For you, Lord, are good, and ready to forgive; Abundant in lovingkindness to all those who call on you.
⁶ Hear, Yahweh, my prayer. Listen to the voice of my petitions.
⁷ In the day of my trouble I will call on you, For you will answer me.
⁸ There is no one like you among the gods, Lord, Nor any deeds like your deeds.
⁹ All nations you have made will come and worship before you, Lord. They shall glorify your name.
¹⁰ For you are great, and do wondrous things. You are God alone.
¹¹ Teach me your way, Yahweh. I will walk in your truth. Make my heart undivided to fear your name.
¹² I will praise you, Lord my God, with my whole heart. I will glorify your name forevermore.
¹³ For your lovingkindness is great toward me. You have delivered my soul from the lowest Sheol.

¹⁴ God, the proud have risen up against me. A company of violent men have sought after my soul, And they don't hold regard for you before them.
¹⁵ But you, Lord, are a merciful and gracious God, Slow to anger, and abundant in lovingkindness and truth.
¹⁶ Turn to me, and have mercy on me! Give your strength to your servant. Save the son of your handmaid.
¹⁷ Show me a sign of your goodness, That those who hate me may see it, and be put to shame, Because you, Yahweh, have helped me, and comforted me. Psalm 87 A Psalm by the sons of Korah; a Song.

Psalms 87

¹ His foundation is in the holy mountains.
² Yahweh loves the gates of Zion More than all the dwellings of Jacob.
³ Glorious things are spoken about you, city of God. Selah.
⁴ I will record Rahab and Babylon among those who acknowledge me. Behold, Philistia, Tyre, and also Ethiopia: "This one was born there."
⁵ Yes, of Zion it will be said, "This one and that one was born in her;" The Most High himself will establish her.
⁶ Yahweh will count, when he writes up the peoples, "This one was born there." Selah.
⁷ Those who sing as well as those who dance say, "All my springs are in you." Psalm 88 A Song. A Psalm by the

sons of Korah. For the Chief Musician. To the tune of "The Suffering of Affliction." A contemplation by Heman, the Ezrahite.

Psalms 88

¹ Yahweh, the God of my salvation, I have cried day and night before you.
² Let my prayer enter into your presence. Turn your ear to my cry.
³ For my soul is full of troubles. My life draws near to Sheol.
⁴ I am counted among those who go down into the pit. I am like a man who has no help,
⁵ Set apart among the dead, Like the slain who lie in the grave, Whom you remember no more. They are cut off from your hand.
⁶ You have laid me in the lowest pit, In the darkest depths.
⁷ Your wrath lies heavily on me. You have afflicted me with all your waves. Selah.
⁸ You have taken my friends from me. You have made me an abomination to them. I am confined, and I can`t escape.
⁹ My eyes are dim from grief. I have called on you daily, Yahweh. I have spread out my hands to you.

¹⁰ Do you show wonders to the dead? Do the dead rise up and praise you? Selah.
¹¹ Is your lovingkindness declared in the grave? Or your faithfulness in Destruction?
¹² Are your wonders made known in the dark? Or your righteousness in the land of forgetfulness?
¹³ But to you, Yahweh, I have cried. In the morning, my prayer comes before you.
¹⁴ Yahweh, why do you reject my soul? Why do you hide your face from me?
¹⁵ I am afflicted and ready to die from my youth up. While I suffer your terrors, I am distracted.
¹⁶ Your fierce wrath has gone over me. Your terrors have cut me off.
¹⁷ They came around me like water all day long. They completely engulfed me.
¹⁸ You have put lover and friend far from me, And my friends into darkness. Psalm 89 A contemplation by Ethan, the Ezrahite.

Psalms 89

¹ I will sing of the lovingkindness of Yahweh forever. With my mouth, I will make known your faithfulness to all generations.
² I indeed declare, "Love stands firm forever. You established the heavens. Your faithfulness is in them."

³ "I have made a covenant with my chosen one, I have sworn to David, my servant,
⁴ `I will establish your seed forever, And build up your throne to all generations.`" Selah.
⁵ The heavens will praise your wonders, Yahweh; Your faithfulness also in the assembly of the holy ones.
⁶ For who in the skies can be compared to Yahweh? Who among the sons of the heavenly beings is like Yahweh,
⁷ A very awesome God in the council of the holy ones, To be feared above all those who are around him?
⁸ Yahweh, God of hosts, who is a mighty one, like you? Yah, your faithfulness is around you.
⁹ You rule the pride of the sea. When its waves rise up, you calm them.
¹⁰ You have broken Rahab in pieces, like one of the slain. You have scattered your enemies with your mighty arm.
¹¹ The heavens are yours, the earth also is yours; The world and its fullness. You have founded them.
¹² The north and the south, you have created them. Tabor and Hermon rejoice in your name.
¹³ You have a mighty arm. Your hand is strong, and your right hand is exalted.
¹⁴ Righteousness and justice are the foundation of your throne. Lovingkindness and truth go before your face.
¹⁵ Blessed are the people who learn to acclaim you. They walk in the light of your presence, Yahweh.
¹⁶ In your name do they rejoice all day. In your righteousness, they are exalted.
¹⁷ For you are the glory of their strength. In your favor, our horn will be exalted.

¹⁸ For our shield belongs to Yahweh; Our king to the Holy One of Israel.
¹⁹ Then you spoke in vision to your saints, And said, "I have bestowed strength on the warrior. I have exalted a young man from the people.
²⁰ I have found David, my servant. I have anointed him with my holy oil,
²¹ With whom my hand shall be established. My arm will also strengthen him.
²² No enemy will tax him. No wicked man will oppress him.
²³ I will beat down his adversaries before him, And strike those who hate him.
²⁴ But my faithfulness and my lovingkindness will be with him. In my name, his horn will be exalted.
²⁵ I will set his hand also on the sea, And his right hand on the rivers.
²⁶ He will call to me, `You are my Father, My God, and the rock of my salvation!`
²⁷ I will also appoint him my firstborn, The highest of the kings of the earth.
²⁸ I will keep my lovingkindness for him forevermore. My covenant will stand firm with him.
²⁹ I will also make his seed endure forever, And his throne as the days of heaven.
³⁰ If his children forsake my law, And don`t walk in my ordinances;
³¹ If they break my statutes, And don`t keep my commandments;

³² Then I will punish their sin with the rod, And their iniquity with stripes.
³³ But I will not completely take my lovingkindness from him, Nor allow my faithfulness to fail.
³⁴ I will not break my covenant, Nor alter what my lips have uttered.
³⁵ Once have I sworn by my holiness, I will not lie to David.
³⁶ His seed will endure forever, His throne like the sun before me.
³⁷ It will be established forever like the moon, The faithful witness in the sky." Selah.
³⁸ But you have rejected and spurned. You have been angry with your anointed.
³⁹ You have renounced the covenant of your servant. You have defiled his crown in the dust.
⁴⁰ You have broken down all his hedges. You have brought his strongholds to ruin.
⁴¹ All who pass by the way rob him. He has become a reproach to his neighbors.
⁴² You have exalted the right hand of his adversaries. You have made all of his enemies rejoice.
⁴³ Yes, you turn back the edge of his sword, And haven't supported him in battle.
⁴⁴ You have ended his splendor, And thrown his throne down to the ground.
⁴⁵ You have shortened the days of his youth. You have covered him with shame. Selah.
⁴⁶ How long, Yahweh? Will you hide yourself forever? Will your wrath burn like fire?

⁴⁷ Remember how short my time is! For what vanity have you created all the children of men!
⁴⁸ What man is he who shall live and not see death, Who shall deliver his soul from the power of Sheol? Selah.
⁴⁹ Lord, where are your former lovingkindnesses, Which you swore to David in your faithfulness?
⁵⁰ Remember, Lord, the reproach of your servants, How I bear in my heart the taunts of all the mighty peoples,
⁵¹ With which your enemies have mocked, Yahweh, With which they have mocked the footsteps of your anointed one.
⁵² Blessed be Yahweh forevermore. Amen, and Amen.
BOOK IV Psalm 90 A Prayer by Moses, the man of God.

Psalms 90

¹ Lord, you have been our dwelling place In all generations.
² Before the mountains were brought forth, Or ever you had formed the earth and the world, Even from everlasting to everlasting, you are God.
³ You turn man to destruction, saying, "Return, you children of men."
⁴ For a thousand years in your sight Are but as yesterday when it is past, As a watch in the night.
⁵ You sweep them away as they sleep. In the morning they sprout like new grass.

6 In the morning it sprouts and springs up. By evening, it is withered and dry.
7 For we are consumed in your anger. We are troubled in your wrath.
8 You have set our iniquities before you, Our secret sins in the light of your presence.
9 For all our days have passed away in your wrath. We bring our years to an end as a sigh.
10 The days of our years are seventy, Or even by reason of strength eighty years; Yet their pride is but labor and sorrow, For it passes quickly, and we fly away.
11 Who knows the power of your anger, Your wrath according to the fear that is due to you?
12 So teach us to number our days, That we may gain a heart of wisdom.
13 Relent, Yahweh! How long? Have compassion on your servants.
14 Satisfy us in the morning with your lovingkindness, That we may rejoice and be glad all our days.
15 Make us glad for as many days as you have afflicted us, For as many years as we have seen evil.
16 Let your work appear to your servants; Your glory to their children.
17 Let the favor of the Lord our God be on us; Establish the work of our hands for us; Yes, establish the work of our hands. Psalm 91

Psalms 91

¹ He who dwells in the secret place of the Most High Will rest in the shadow of the Almighty.

² I will say of Yahweh, "He is my refuge and my fortress; My God, in whom I trust."

³ For he will deliver you from the snare of the fowler, From the deadly pestilence.

⁴ He will cover you with his pinions, Under his wings you will take refuge. His truth is a shield and a buckler.

⁵ You will not be afraid of the terror by night, Nor of the arrow that flies by day;

⁶ Nor of the pestilence that walks in darkness, Nor for the destruction that wastes at noonday.

⁷ A thousand shall fall at your side, And ten thousand at your right hand; But it will not come near you.

⁸ You will only look with your eyes, And see the reward of the wicked.

⁹ For you, Yahweh, are my refuge! You have made the Most High your habitation.

¹⁰ No evil will happen to you, Neither shall any plague come near your tent.

¹¹ For he will give his angels charge over you, To guard you in all your ways.

¹² They will bear you up in their hands, So that you won`t dash your foot against a stone.

¹³ You will tread on the lion and cobra. You will trample the young lion and the serpent underfoot.

¹⁴ Because he has set his love on me, therefore I will deliver him. I will set him on high, because he has known my name.
¹⁵ He will call on me, and I will answer him. I will be with him in trouble. I will deliver him, and honor him.
¹⁶ I will satisfy him with long life, And show him my salvation. Psalm 92 A Psalm. A song for the Sabbath day.

Psalms 92

¹ It is a good thing to give thanks to Yahweh, To sing praises to your name, Most High;
² To proclaim your lovingkindness in the morning, And your faithfulness every night,
³ With the ten-stringed lute, with the harp, And with the melody of the lyre.
⁴ For you, Yahweh, have made me glad through your work. I will triumph in the works of your hands.
⁵ How great are your works, Yahweh! Your thoughts are very deep.
⁶ A senseless man doesn`t know, Neither does a fool understand this:
⁷ Though the wicked spring up as the grass, And all the evil-doers flourish, They will be destroyed forever.
⁸ But you, Yahweh, are on high forevermore.
⁹ For, behold, your enemies, Yahweh, For, behold, your enemies shall perish. All the evil-doers will be scattered.

¹⁰ But you have exalted my horn like that of the wild ox. I am anointed with fresh oil.
¹¹ My eye has also seen my enemies, My ears have heard of the evil-doers who rise up against me.
¹² The righteous shall flourish like the palm tree. He will grow like a cedar in Lebanon.
¹³ They are planted in Yahweh`s house. They will flourish in our God`s courts.
¹⁴ They will still bring forth fruit in old age. They will be full of sap and green,
¹⁵ To show that Yahweh is upright. He is my rock, and there is no unrighteousness in him. Psalm 93

Psalms 93

¹ Yahweh reigns! He is clothed with majesty! Yahweh is armed with strength. The world also is established. It can`t be moved.
² Your throne is established from long ago. You are from everlasting.
³ The floods have lifted up, Yahweh, The floods have lifted up their voice. The floods lift up their waves.
⁴ Above the voices of many waters, The mighty breakers of the sea, Yahweh on high is mighty.
⁵ Your statutes stand firm. Holiness adorns your house, Yahweh, forevermore. Psalm 94

Psalms 94

¹ Yahweh, you God to whom vengeance belongs, You God to whom vengeance belongs, shine forth.
² Rise up, you judge of the earth. Pay back the proud what they deserve.
³ Yahweh, how long will the wicked, How long will the wicked triumph?
⁴ They pour out arrogant words. All the evil-doers boast.
⁵ They break your people in pieces, Yahweh, And afflict your heritage.
⁶ They kill the widow and the alien, And murder the fatherless.
⁷ They say, "Yah will not see, Neither will Jacob`s God consider."
⁸ Consider, you senseless among the people; You fools, when will you be wise?
⁹ He who implanted the ear, won`t he hear? He who formed the eye, won`t he see?
¹⁰ He who disciplines the nations, won`t he punish? He who teaches man knows.
¹¹ Yahweh knows the thoughts of man, That they are futile.
¹² Blessed is the man whom you discipline, Yah, And teach out of your law;
¹³ That you may give him rest from the days of adversity, Until the pit is dug for the wicked.
¹⁴ For Yahweh won`t reject his people, Neither will he forsake his inheritance.

15 For judgment will return to righteousness. All the upright in heart shall follow it.
16 Who will rise up for me against the wicked? Who will stand up for me against the evil-doers?
17 Unless Yahweh had been my help, My soul would have soon lived in silence.
18 When I said, "My foot is slipping!" Your lovingkindness, Yahweh, held me up.
19 In the multitude of my thoughts within me, Your comforts delight my soul.
20 Shall the throne of wickedness have fellowship with you, Which brings about mischief by statute?
21 They gather themselves together against the soul of the righteous, And condemn the innocent blood.
22 But Yahweh has been my high tower, My God, the rock of my refuge.
23 He has brought on them their own iniquity, And will cut them off in their own wickedness. Yahweh, our God, will cut them off. Psalm 95

Psalms 95

1 Oh come, let us sing to Yahweh. Let us make a joyful noise to the rock of our salvation!
2 Let us come before his presence with thanksgiving. Let us make a joyful noise to him with psalms!
3 For Yahweh is a great God, A great King above all gods.

⁴ In his hand are the deep places of the earth. The heights of the mountains are also his.
⁵ The sea is his, and he made it. His hands formed the dry land.
⁶ Oh come, let us worship and bow down. Let us kneel before Yahweh, our Maker,
⁷ For he is our God. We are the people of his pasture, and the sheep of his hand. Today, oh that you would hear his voice!
⁸ Don`t harden your heart, as at Meribah, As in the day of Massah in the wilderness,
⁹ When your fathers tempted me, Tested me, and saw my work.
¹⁰ Forty long years I was grieved with that generation, And said, "It is a people that errs in their heart. They have not known my ways."
¹¹ Therefore I swore in my wrath, "They won`t enter into my rest." Psalm 96

Psalms 96

¹ Sing to Yahweh a new song! Sing to Yahweh, all the earth.
² Sing to Yahweh! Bless his name. Proclaim his salvation from day to day.
³ Declare his glory among the nations, His marvelous works among all the peoples.

⁴ For great is Yahweh, and greatly to be praised! He is to be feared above all gods.
⁵ For all the gods of the peoples are idols, But Yahweh made the heavens.
⁶ Honor and majesty are before him. Strength and beauty are in his sanctuary.
⁷ Ascribe to Yahweh, you families of nations, Ascribe to Yahweh glory and strength.
⁸ Ascribe to Yahweh the glory due to his name. Bring an offering, and come into his courts.
⁹ Worship Yahweh in holy array. Tremble before him, all the earth.
¹⁰ Say among the nations, "Yahweh reigns." The world is also established. It can`t be moved. He will judge the peoples with equity.
¹¹ Let the heavens be glad, and let the earth rejoice. Let the sea roar, and the fullness of it!
¹² Let the field exult, and all that is therein. Then shall all the trees of the wood sing for joy
¹³ Before Yahweh; for he comes, For he comes to judge the earth. He will judge the world with righteousness, The peoples with his truth. Psalm 97

Psalms 97

¹ Yahweh reigns! Let the earth rejoice. Let the multitude of islands be glad.

2 Clouds and darkness are around him. Righteousness and justice are the foundation of his throne.
3 A fire goes before him, And burns up his adversaries on every side.
4 His lightning lights up the world; The earth sees, and trembles.
5 The mountains melt like wax at the presence of Yahweh, At the presence of the Lord of the whole earth.
6 The heavens declare his righteousness. All the peoples have seen his glory.
7 Let all them be put to shame who serve engraved images, Who boast in their idols. Worship him, all you gods!
8 Zion heard and was glad. The daughters of Judah rejoiced, Because of your judgments, Yahweh.
9 For you, Yahweh, are most high above all the earth. You are exalted far above all gods.
10 You who love Yahweh, hate evil. He preserves the souls of his saints. He delivers them out of the hand of the wicked.
11 Light is sown for the righteous, And gladness for the upright in heart.
12 Be glad in Yahweh, you righteous people! Give thanks to his holy Name. Psalm 98 A Psalm.

Psalms 98

¹ Sing to Yahweh a new song, For he has done marvelous things! His right hand, and his holy arm, have worked salvation for him.
² Yahweh has made known his salvation. He has openly shown his righteousness in the sight of the nations.
³ He has remembered his lovingkindness and his faithfulness toward the house of Israel. All the ends of the earth have seen the salvation of our God.
⁴ Make a joyful noise to Yahweh, all the earth! Burst out and sing for joy, yes, sing praises!
⁵ Sing praises to Yahweh with the harp, With the harp and the voice of melody.
⁶ With trumpets and sound of the ram`s horn. Make a joyful noise before the King, Yahweh.
⁷ Let the sea roar with its fullness; The world, and those who dwell therein.
⁸ Let the rivers clap their hands. Let the mountains sing for joy together.
⁹ Let them sing before Yahweh, For he comes to judge the earth. He will judge the world with righteousness, And the peoples with equity. Psalm 99

Psalms 99

¹ Yahweh reigns! Let the peoples tremble. He sits enthroned among the cherubim. Let the earth be moved.

² Yahweh is great in Zion. He is high above all the peoples.
³ Let them praise your great and awesome name. He is Holy!
⁴ The King`s strength also loves justice. You do establish equity. You execute justice and righteousness in Jacob.
⁵ Exalt Yahweh our God. Worship at his footstool. He is Holy!
⁶ Moses and Aaron were among his priests, Samuel among those who call on his name; They called on Yahweh, and he answered them.
⁷ He spoke to them in the pillar of cloud. They kept his testimonies, The statute that he gave them.
⁸ You answered them, Yahweh our God. You are a God who forgave them, Although you took vengeance for their doings.
⁹ Exalt Yahweh, our God. Worship at his holy hill, For Yahweh, our God, is holy! Psalm 100 A Psalm of thanksgiving.

Psalms 100

¹ Make a joyful noise to Yahweh, all you lands!
² Serve Yahweh with gladness. Come before his presence with singing.

³ Know that Yahweh, he is God. It is he who has made us, and we are his. We are his people, and the sheep of his pasture.
⁴ Enter into his gates with thanksgiving, Into his courts with praise. Give thanks to him, and bless his name.
⁵ For Yahweh is good. His lovingkindness endures forever, His faithfulness to all generations. Psalm 101 A Psalm by David.

Psalms 101

¹ I will sing of lovingkindness and justice. To you, Yahweh, I will sing praises.
² I will be careful to live a blameless life. When will you come to me? I will walk within my house with a blameless heart.
³ I will set no vile thing before my eyes. I hate the deeds of faithless men. They will not cling to me.
⁴ A perverse heart will be far from me. I will have nothing to do with evil.
⁵ I will silence whoever secretly slanders his neighbor. I won't tolerate one who is haughty and conceited.
⁶ My eyes will be on the faithful of the land, That they may dwell with me. He who walks in a perfect way, He will serve me.
⁷ He who practices deceit won't dwell within my house. He who speaks falsehood won't be established before my eyes.

⁸ Morning by morning, I will destroy all the wicked of the land; To cut off all the workers of iniquity from Yahweh`s city. Psalm 102 A Prayer of the afflicted, when he is overwhelmed and pours out his complaint before Yahweh.

Psalms 102

¹ Hear my prayer, Yahweh! Let my cry come to you.
² Don`t hide your face from me in the day of my distress. Turn your ear to me. Answer me quickly in the day when I call.
³ For my days consume away like smoke. My bones are burned as a firebrand.
⁴ My heart is blighted like grass, and withered, For I forget to eat my bread.
⁵ By reason of the voice of my groaning, My bones stick to my skin.
⁶ I am like a pelican of the wilderness. I have become as an owl of the waste places.
⁷ I watch, and have become like a sparrow that is alone on the housetop.
⁸ My enemies reproach me all day. Those who are mad at me use my name as a curse.
⁹ For I have eaten ashes like bread, And mingled my drink with tears,
¹⁰ Because of your indignation and your wrath, For you have taken me up, and thrown me away.

¹¹ My days are like a long shadow. I have withered like grass.
¹² But you, Yahweh, will abide forever; Your renown endures to all generations.
¹³ You will arise and have mercy on Zion; For it is time to have pity on her. Yes, the set time has come.
¹⁴ For your servants take pleasure in her stones, And have pity on her dust.
¹⁵ So the nations will fear the name of Yahweh; All the kings of the earth your glory.
¹⁶ For Yahweh has built up Zion. He has appeared in his glory.
¹⁷ He has responded to the prayer of the destitute, And has not despised their prayer.
¹⁸ This will be written for the generation to come. A people which will be created will praise Yah.
¹⁹ For he has looked down from the height of his sanctuary. From heaven, Yahweh saw the earth;
²⁰ To hear the groans of the prisoner; To free those who are condemned to death;
²¹ That men may declare the name of Yahweh in Zion, And his praise in Jerusalem;
²² When the peoples are gathered together, The kingdoms, to serve Yahweh.
²³ He weakened my strength along the course. He shortened my days.
²⁴ I said, "My God, don`t take me away in the midst of my days. Your years are throughout all generations.
²⁵ Of old, you laid the foundation of the earth. The heavens are the work of your hands.

²⁶ They will perish, but you will endure. Yes, all of them will wear out like a garment. You will change them like a cloak, and they will be changed.
²⁷ But you are the same. Your years will have no end.
²⁸ The children of your servants will continue. Their seed will be established before you." Psalm 103 By David.

Psalms 103

¹ Praise Yahweh, my soul! All that is within me, praise his holy name!
² Praise Yahweh, my soul, And don't forget all his benefits;
³ Who forgives all your sins; Who heals all your diseases;
⁴ Who redeems your life from destruction; Who crowns you with lovingkindness and tender mercies;
⁵ Who satisfies your desire with good things, So that your youth is renewed like the eagle's.
⁶ Yahweh executes righteous acts, And justice for all who are oppressed.
⁷ He made known his ways to Moses, His deeds to the children of Israel.
⁸ Yahweh is merciful and gracious, Slow to anger, and abundant in lovingkindness.
⁹ He will not always accuse; Neither will he stay angry forever.
¹⁰ He has not dealt with us according to our sins, Nor rewarded us for our iniquities.

¹¹ For as the heavens are high above the earth, So great is his lovingkindness toward those who fear him.

¹² As far as the east is from the west, So far has he removed our transgressions from us.

¹³ Like a father has compassion on his children, So Yahweh has compassion on those who fear him.

¹⁴ For he knows how we are made. He remembers that we are dust.

¹⁵ As for man, his days are like grass. As a flower of the field, so he flourishes.

¹⁶ For the wind passes over it, and it is gone. Its place remembers it no more.

¹⁷ But Yahweh's lovingkindness is from everlasting to everlasting with those who fear him, His righteousness to children's children;

¹⁸ To those who keep his covenant, To those who remember to obey his precepts.

¹⁹ Yahweh has established his throne in the heavens. His kingdom rules over all.

²⁰ Praise Yahweh, you angels of his, Who are mighty in strength, who fulfill his word, Obeying the voice of his word.

²¹ Praise Yahweh, all you hosts of his, You servants of his, who do his pleasure.

²² Praise Yahweh, all you works of his, In all places of his dominion. Praise Yahweh, my soul. Psalm 104

Psalms 104

¹ Bless Yahweh, my soul. Yahweh, my God, you are very great. You are clothed with honor and majesty.
² He covers himself with light as with a garment. He stretches out the heavens like a curtain.
³ He lays the beams of his chambers in the waters. He makes the clouds his chariot. He walks on the wings of the wind.
⁴ He makes his messengers winds; His servants flames of fire.
⁵ He laid the foundations of the earth, That it should not be moved forever.
⁶ You covered it with the deep as with a cloak. The waters stood above the mountains.
⁷ At your rebuke they fled. At the voice of your thunder they hurried away.
⁸ The mountains rose, The valleys sank down, To the place which you had assigned to them.
⁹ You have set a boundary that they may not pass over; That they don't turn again to cover the earth.
¹⁰ He sends forth springs into the valleys. They run among the mountains.
¹¹ They give drink to every animal of the field. The wild donkeys quench their thirst.
¹² The birds of the sky nest by them. They sing among the branches.
¹³ He waters the mountains from his chambers. The earth is filled with the fruit of your works.

¹⁴ He causes the grass to grow for the cattle, And plants for man to cultivate, That he may bring forth food out of the earth:

¹⁵ Wine that makes glad the heart of man, Oil to make his face to shine, And bread that strengthens man`s heart.

¹⁶ Yahweh`s trees are well watered, The cedars of Lebanon, which he has planted;

¹⁷ Where the birds make their nests. The stork makes its home in the fir trees.

¹⁸ The high mountains are for the wild goats. The rocks are a refuge for the rock badgers.

¹⁹ He appointed the moon for seasons. The sun knows when to set.

²⁰ You make darkness, and it is night, In which all the animals of the forest prowl.

²¹ The young lions roar after their prey, And seek their food from God.

²² The sun rises, and they steal away, And lay down in their dens.

²³ Man goes forth to his work, To his labor until the evening.

²⁴ Yahweh, how many are your works! In wisdom have you made them all. The earth is full of your riches.

²⁵ There is the sea, great and wide, In which are innumerable living things, Both small and great animals.

²⁶ There the ships go, And leviathan, whom you formed to play there.

²⁷ These all wait for you, That you may give them their food in due season.

²⁸ You give to them; they gather. You open your hand; they are satisfied with good.
²⁹ You hide your face: they are troubled; You take away their breath: they die, and return to the dust.
³⁰ You send forth your Spirit: they are created. You renew the face of the ground.
³¹ Let the glory of Yahweh endure forever. Let Yahweh rejoice in his works.
³² He looks at the earth, and it trembles. He touches the mountains, and they smoke.
³³ I will sing to Yahweh as long as I live. I will sing praise to my God while I have any being.
³⁴ Let your meditation be sweet to him. I will rejoice in Yahweh.
³⁵ Let sinners be consumed out of the earth. Let the wicked be no more. Bless Yahweh, my soul. Praise Yah! Psalm 105

Psalms 105

¹ Give thanks to Yahweh! Call on his name! Make his doings known among the peoples.
² Sing to him, sing praises to him! Tell of all his marvelous works.
³ Glory in his holy name. Let the heart of them rejoice who seek Yahweh.
⁴ Seek Yahweh and his strength. Seek his face forever more.

⁵ Remember his marvelous works that he has done; His wonders, and the judgments of his mouth,
⁶ You seed of Abraham, his servant, You children of Jacob, his chosen ones.
⁷ He is Yahweh, our God. His judgments are in all the earth.
⁸ He has remembered his covenant forever, The word which he commanded to a thousand generations,
⁹ The covenant which he made with Abraham, His oath to Isaac,
¹⁰ And confirmed the same to Jacob for a statute;
To Israel for an everlasting covenant,
¹¹ Saying, "To you I will give the land of Canaan, The lot of your inheritance;"
¹² When they were but a few men in number, Yes, very few, and sojourners in it.
¹³ They went about from nation to nation, From one kingdom to another people.
¹⁴ He allowed no one to do them wrong. Yes, he reproved kings for their sakes,
¹⁵ "Don`t touch my anointed ones. Do my prophets no harm."
¹⁶ He called for a famine on the land. He destroyed the food supplies.
¹⁷ He sent a man before them. Joseph was sold for a slave.
¹⁸ They bruised his feet with shackles. His neck was locked in irons,
¹⁹ Until the time that his word happened, And Yahweh`s word proved him true.

20 The king sent and freed him; Even the ruler of peoples, and let him go free.
21 He made him lord of his house, And ruler of all of his possessions;
22 To discipline his princes at his pleasure, And to teach his elders wisdom.
23 Israel also came into Egypt. Jacob sojourned in the land of Ham.
24 He increased his people greatly, And made them stronger than their adversaries.
25 He turned their heart to hate his people, To conspire against his servants.
26 He sent Moses, his servant, And Aaron, whom he had chosen.
27 They performed miracles among them, And wonders in the land of Ham.
28 He sent darkness, and made it dark. They didn`t rebel against his words.
29 He turned their waters into blood, And killed their fish.
30 Their land swarmed with frogs, Even in the chambers of their kings.
31 He spoke, and swarms of flies came, And lice in all their borders.
32 He gave them hail for rain, With lightning in their land.
33 He struck their vines and also their fig trees, And shattered the trees of their country.
34 He spoke, and the locusts came, And the grasshoppers, without number,
35 Ate up every plant in their land; Ate up the fruit of their ground.

36 He struck also all the firstborn in their land, The chief of all their strength.
37 He brought them forth with silver and gold. There was not one feeble person among his tribes.
38 Egypt was glad when they departed, For the fear of them had fallen on them.
39 He spread a cloud for a covering, Fire to give light in the night.
40 They asked, and he brought quails, And satisfied them with the bread of the sky.
41 He opened the rock, and waters gushed out. They ran as a river in the dry places.
42 For he remembered his holy word, And Abraham, his servant.
43 He brought forth his people with joy, His chosen with singing.
44 He gave them the lands of the nations. They took the labor of the peoples in possession,
45 That they might keep his statutes, And observe his laws. Praise Yah! Psalm 106

Psalms 106

1 Praise Yahweh! Give thanks to Yahweh, for he is good, For his lovingkindness endures forever.
2 Who can utter the mighty acts of Yahweh, Or fully declare all his praise?

³ Blessed are those who keep justice, He who does righteousness at all times.
⁴ Remember me, Yahweh, with the favor that you show to your people. Visit me with your salvation,
⁵ That I may see the prosperity of your chosen, That I may rejoice in the gladness of your nation, That I may glory with your inheritance.
⁶ We have sinned with our fathers. We have committed iniquity. We have done wickedly.
⁷ Our fathers didn`t understand your wonders in Egypt. They didn`t remember the multitude of your lovingkindnesses, But were rebellious at the sea, even at the Red Sea.
⁸ Nevertheless he saved them for his name`s sake, That he might make his mighty power known.
⁹ He rebuked the Red Sea also, and it was dried up; So he led them through the depths, as through a desert.
¹⁰ He saved them from the hand of him who hated them, And redeemed them from the hand of the enemy.
¹¹ The waters covered their adversaries. There was not one of them left.
¹² Then they believed his words. They sang his praise.
¹³ They soon forgot his works. They didn`t wait for his counsel,
¹⁴ But gave in to craving in the desert, And tested God in the wasteland.
¹⁵ He gave them their request, But sent leanness into their soul.
¹⁶ They envied Moses also in the camp, And Aaron, Yahweh`s saint.

17 The earth opened and swallowed up Dathan, And covered the company of Abiram.
18 A fire was kindled in their company. The flame burned up the wicked.
19 They made a calf in Horeb, And worshipped a molten image.
20 Thus they exchanged their glory For an image of a bull that eats grass.
21 They forgot God, their Savior, Who had done great things in Egypt,
22 Wondrous works in the land of Ham, And awesome things by the Red Sea.
23 Therefore he said that he would destroy them, Had Moses, his chosen, not stood before him in the breach, To turn away his wrath, so that he wouldn't destroy them.
24 Yes, they despised the pleasant land. They didn't believe his word,
25 But murmured in their tents, And didn't listen to the voice of Yahweh.
26 Therefore he swore to them That he would overthrow them in the wilderness,
27 That he would overthrow their seed among the nations, And scatter them in the lands.
28 They joined themselves also to Baal-peor, And ate the sacrifices of the dead.
29 Thus they provoked him to anger with their deeds. The plague broke in on them.
30 Then Phinehas stood up, and executed judgment, So the plague was stopped.

31 That was credited to him for righteousness, To all generations forevermore.
32 They angered him also at the waters of Meribah, So that Moses was troubled for their sakes;
33 Because they were rebellious against his spirit, He spoke rashly with his lips.
34 They didn`t destroy the peoples, As Yahweh commanded them,
35 But mingled themselves with the nations, Learned their works.
36 They served their idols, Which became a snare to them.
37 Yes, they sacrificed their sons and their daughters to demons.
38 They shed innocent blood, Even the blood of their sons and of their daughters, Whom they sacrificed to the idols of Canaan. The land was polluted with blood.
39 Thus were they defiled with their works, And prostituted themselves in their deeds.
40 Therefore the wrath of Yahweh was kindled against his people. He abhorred his inheritance.
41 He gave them into the hand of the nations. Those who hated them ruled over them.
42 Their enemies also oppressed them. They were brought into subjection under their hand.
43 Many times he delivered them, But they were rebellious in their counsel, And were brought low in their iniquity.
44 Nevertheless he regarded their distress, When he heard their cry.

⁴⁵ He remembered for them his covenant, And repented according to the multitude of his lovingkindnesses.
⁴⁶ He made them also to be pitied By all those who carried them captive.
⁴⁷ Save us, Yahweh, our God, Gather us from among the nations, To give thanks to your holy name, To triumph in your praise!
⁴⁸ Blessed be Yahweh, the God of Israel, From everlasting even to everlasting! Let all the people say, "Amen." Praise Yah! BOOK V Psalm 107

Psalms 107

¹ Give thanks to Yahweh, For he is good, For his lovingkindness endures forever.
² Let the redeemed by Yahweh say so, Whom he has redeemed from the hand of the adversary,
³ Gathered out of the lands, From the east and from the west, From the north and from the south.
⁴ They wandered in the wilderness in a desert way. They found no city to live in.
⁵ Hungry and thirsty, Their soul fainted in them.
⁶ Then they cried to Yahweh in their trouble, And he delivered them out of their distresses,
⁷ He led them also by a straight way, That they might go to a city to live in.
⁸ Let them praise Yahweh for his lovingkindness, For his wonderful works to the children of men!

⁹ For he satisfies the longing soul. He fills the hungry soul with good.
¹⁰ Some sat in darkness and in the shadow of death, Being bound in affliction and iron,
¹¹ Because they rebelled against the words of God, And condemned the counsel of the Most High.
¹² Therefore he brought down their heart with labor. They fell down, and there was none to help.
¹³ Then they cried to Yahweh in their trouble, And he saved them out of their distresses.
¹⁴ He brought them out of darkness and the shadow of death, And broke their bonds in sunder.
¹⁵ Let them praise Yahweh for his lovingkindness, For his wonderful works to the children of men!
¹⁶ For he has broken the gates of brass, And cut through bars of iron.
¹⁷ Fools are afflicted because of their disobedience, And because of their iniquities.
¹⁸ Their soul abhors all kinds of food. They draw near to the gates of death.
¹⁹ Then they cry to Yahweh in their trouble, He saves them out of their distresses.
²⁰ He sends his word, and heals them, And delivers them from their graves.
²¹ Let them praise Yahweh for his lovingkindness, For his wonderful works to the children of men!
²² Let them offer the sacrifices of thanksgiving, And declare his works with singing.
²³ Those who go down to the sea in ships, Who do business in great waters;

²⁴ These see Yahweh's works, And his wonders in the deep.
²⁵ For he commands, and raises the stormy wind, Which lifts up its waves.
²⁶ They mount up to the sky; they go down again to the depths. Their soul melts away because of trouble.
²⁷ They reel back and forth, and stagger like a drunken man, And are at their wits' end.
²⁸ Then they cry to Yahweh in their trouble, He brings them out of their distress.
²⁹ He makes the storm a calm, So that its waves are still.
³⁰ Then are they glad because it is calm, So he brings them to their desired haven.
³¹ Let them praise Yahweh for his lovingkindness, For his wonderful works to the children of men!
³² Let them exalt him also in the assembly of the people, And praise him in the seat of the elders.
³³ He turns rivers into a desert, Water springs into a thirsty ground,
³⁴ And a fruitful land into a salt waste, For the wickedness of those who dwell in it.
³⁵ He turns a desert into a pool of water, And a dry land into water springs.
³⁶ There he makes the hungry to live, That they may prepare a city to live in,
³⁷ Sow fields, plant vineyards, And reap the fruits of increase.
³⁸ He blesses them also, so that they are multiplied greatly. He doesn't allow their cattle to decrease.

[39] Again, they are diminished and bowed down Through oppression, trouble, and sorrow.
[40] He pours contempt on princes, And causes them to wander in a trackless waste.
[41] Yet he lifts the needy out of their affliction, And increases their families like a flock.
[42] The upright will see it, and be glad. All the wicked will shut their mouths.
[43] Whoever is wise will pay attention to these things. They will consider the lovingkindnesses of Yahweh.
Psalm 108 A Song. A Psalm by David.

Psalms 108

[1] My heart is steadfast, God. I will sing and I will make music with my soul.
[2] Wake up, harp and lyre! I will wake up the dawn.
[3] I will give thanks to you, Yahweh, among the nations. I will sing praises to you among the peoples.
[4] For your lovingkindness is great above the heavens. Your faithfulness reaches to the skies.
[5] Be exalted, God, above the heavens, Let your glory be over all the earth.
[6] That your beloved may be delivered, Save with your right hand, and answer us.
[7] God has spoken from his sanctuary: "In triumph, I will divide Shechem, and measure out the valley of Succoth.

⁸ Gilead is mine. Manasseh is mine. Ephraim also is my helmet. Judah is my scepter.
⁹ Moab is my wash pot. I will toss my sandal on Edom. I will shout over Philistia."
¹⁰ Who will bring me into the fortified city? Who has led me to Edom?
¹¹ Haven`t you rejected us, God? You don`t go forth, God, with our armies.
¹² Give us help against the enemy, For the help of man is vain.
¹³ Through God, we will do valiantly. For it is he who will tread down our enemies. Psalm 109 For the Chief Musician. A Psalm by David.

Psalms 109

¹ God of my praise, don`t remain silent,
² For they have opened the mouth of the wicked and the mouth of deceit against me. They have spoken to me with a lying tongue.
³ They have also surrounded me with words of hatred, And fought against me without a cause.
⁴ In return for my love, they are my adversaries; But I am in prayer.
⁵ They have rewarded me evil for good, And hatred for my love.
⁶ Set a wicked man over him. Let an adversary stand at his right hand.

⁷ When he is judged, let him come forth guilty. Let his prayer be turned into sin.
⁸ Let his days be few. Let another take his office.
⁹ Let his children be fatherless, And his wife a widow.
¹⁰ Let his children be wandering beggars. Let them be sought from their ruins.
¹¹ Let the creditor seize all that he has. Let strangers plunder the fruit of his labor.
¹² Let there be none to extend kindness to him, Neither let there be any to have pity on his fatherless children.
¹³ Let his posterity be cut off. In the generation following let their name be blotted out.
¹⁴ Let the iniquity of his fathers be remembered by Yahweh. Don't let the sin of his mother be blotted out.
¹⁵ Let them be before Yahweh continually, That he may cut off the memory of them from the earth;
¹⁶ Because he didn't remember to show kindness, But persecuted the poor and needy man, The broken in heart, to kill them.
¹⁷ Yes, he loved cursing, and it came to him. He didn't delight in blessing, and it was far from him.
¹⁸ He clothed himself also with cursing as with his garment. It came into his inward parts like water, Like oil into his bones.
¹⁹ Let it be to him as the clothing with which he covers himself, For the belt that is always around him.
²⁰ This is the reward of my adversaries from Yahweh, Of those who speak evil against my soul.
²¹ But deal with me, Yahweh the Lord, for your name's sake, Because your lovingkindness is good, deliver me;

²² For I am poor and needy. My heart is wounded within me.
²³ I fade away like an evening shadow. I am shaken off as the locust.
²⁴ My knees are weak through fasting. My body is thin and lacks fat.
²⁵ I have also become a reproach to them. When they see me, they shake their head.
²⁶ Help me, Yahweh, my God. Save me according to your lovingkindness;
²⁷ That they may know that this is your hand; That you, Yahweh, have done it.
²⁸ They may curse, but you bless. When they arise, they will be put to shame, But your servant shall rejoice.
²⁹ Let my adversaries be clothed with dishonor. Let them cover themselves with their own shame as with a robe.
³⁰ I will give great thanks to Yahweh with my mouth. Yes, I will praise him among the multitude.
³¹ For he will stand at the right hand of the needy, To save him from those who judge his soul. Psalm 110 A Psalm by David.

Psalms 110

¹ Yahweh says to my Lord, "Sit at my right hand, Until I make your enemies your footstool for your feet."
² Yahweh will send forth the rod of your strength out of Zion. Rule in the midst of your enemies.

³ Your people offer themselves willingly in the day of your power, In holy array. Out of the womb of the morning, you have the dew of your youth.
⁴ Yahweh has sworn, and will not change his mind: "You are a priest forever in the order of Melchizedek."
⁵ The Lord is at your right hand. He will crush kings in the day of his wrath.
⁶ He will judge among the nations. He will heap up dead bodies. He will crush the ruler of the whole earth.
⁷ He will drink of the brook in the way; Therefore will he lift up his head. Psalm 111

Psalms 111

¹ Praise Yah! I will give thanks to Yahweh with my whole heart, In the council of the upright, and in the congregation.
² The works of Yahweh are great, Pondered by all those who delight in them.
³ His work is honor and majesty. His righteousness endures forever.
⁴ He has caused his wonderful works to be remembered. Yahweh is gracious and merciful.
⁵ He has given food to those who fear him. He always remembers his covenant.

6 He has shown his people the power of his works, In giving them the heritage of the nations.
7 The works of his hands are truth and justice. All his precepts are sure.
8 They are established forever and ever. They are done in truth and uprightness.
9 He has sent redemption to his people. He has ordained his covenant forever. His name is holy and awesome!
10 The fear of Yahweh is the beginning of wisdom. All those who do his work have a good understanding. His praise endures forever! Psalm 112

Psalms 112

1 Praise Yah! Blessed is the man who fears Yahweh, Who delights greatly in his commandments.
2 His seed will be mighty on earth. The generation of the upright will be blessed.
3 Wealth and riches are in his house. His righteousness endures forever.
4 Light dawns in the darkness for the upright, Gracious, merciful, and righteous.
5 It is well with the man who deals graciously and lends. He will maintain his cause in judgment.
6 For he will never be shaken. The righteous will be remembered forever.
7 He will not be afraid of evil news. His heart is steadfast, trusting in Yahweh.

⁸ His heart is established. He will not be afraid in the end when he sees his adversaries.
⁹ He has dispersed, he has given to the poor. His righteousness endures forever. His horn will be exalted with honor.
¹⁰ The wicked will see it, and be grieved. He shall gnash with his teeth, and melt away. The desire of the wicked will perish. Psalm 113

Psalms 113

¹ Praise Yah! Praise, you servants of Yahweh, Praise the name of Yahweh.
² Blessed be the name of Yahweh, From this time forth and forevermore.
³ From the rising of the sun to the going down of the same, Yahweh`s name is to be praised.
⁴ Yahweh is high above all nations, His glory above the heavens.
⁵ Who is like Yahweh, our God, Who has his seat on high,
⁶ Who stoops down to see in heaven and in the earth?
⁷ He raises up the poor out of the dust. Lifts up the needy from the ash heap;
⁸ That he may set him with princes, Even with the princes of his people.
⁹ He settles the barren woman in her home, As a joyful mother of children. Praise Yah! Psalm 114

Psalms 114

¹ When Israel went forth out of Egypt, The house of Jacob from a people of foreign language;
² Judah became his sanctuary, Israel his dominion.
³ The sea saw it, and fled. The Jordan was driven back.
⁴ The mountains skipped like rams, The little hills like lambs.
⁵ What was it, you sea, that you fled? You Jordan, that you turned back?
⁶ You mountains, that you skipped like rams; You little hills, like lambs?
⁷ Tremble, you earth, at the presence of the Lord, At the presence of the God of Jacob,
⁸ Who turned the rock into a pool of water, The flint into a spring of waters. Psalm 115

Psalms 115

¹ Not to us, Yahweh, not to us, But to your name give glory, For your lovingkindness, and for your truth`s sake.
² Why should the nations say, "Where is their God, now?"
³ But our God is in the heavens. He does whatever he pleases.
⁴ Their idols are silver and gold, The work of men`s hands.

⁵ They have mouths, but they don't speak; They have eyes, but they don't see;
⁶ They have ears, but they don't hear; They have noses, but they don't smell;
⁷ They have hands, but they don't feel; They have feet, but they don't walk; Neither do they speak through their throat.
⁸ Those who make them will be like them; Yes, everyone who trusts in them.
⁹ Israel, trust in Yahweh! He is their help and their shield.
¹⁰ House of Aaron, trust in Yahweh! He is their help and their shield.
¹¹ You who fear Yahweh, trust in Yahweh! He is their help and their shield.
¹² Yahweh remembers us. He will bless us. He will bless the house of Israel. He will bless the house of Aaron.
¹³ He will bless those who fear Yahweh, Both small and great.
¹⁴ May Yahweh increase you more and more, You and your children.
¹⁵ Blessed are you by Yahweh, Who made heaven and earth.
¹⁶ The heavens are the heavens of Yahweh; But the earth has he given to the children of men.
¹⁷ The dead don't praise Yah, Neither any who go down into silence;
¹⁸ But we will bless Yah, From this time forth and forevermore. Praise Yah! Psalm 116

Psalms 116

¹ I love Yahweh, because he listens to my voice, And my cries for mercy.
² Because he has turned his ear to me, Therefore I will call on him as long as I live.
³ The cords of death surrounded me, The pains of Sheol got a hold on me. I found trouble and sorrow.
⁴ Then called I on the name of Yahweh: "Yahweh, I beg you, deliver my soul."
⁵ Gracious is Yahweh, and righteous; Yes, our God is merciful.
⁶ Yahweh preserves the simple. I was brought low, and he saved me.
⁷ Return to your rest, my soul, For Yahweh has dealt bountifully with you.
⁸ For you have delivered my soul from death, My eyes from tears, And my feet from falling.
⁹ I will walk before Yahweh in the land of the living.
¹⁰ I believed, therefore I said, "I was greatly afflicted."
¹¹ I said in my haste, "All men are liars."
¹² What will I give to Yahweh for all his benefits toward me?
¹³ I will take the cup of salvation, and call on the name of Yahweh.
¹⁴ I will pay my vows to Yahweh, Yes, in the presence of all his people.
¹⁵ Precious in the sight of Yahweh is the death of his saints.

16 Yahweh, truly I am your servant. I am your servant, the son of your handmaid. You have freed me from my chains.
17 I will offer to you the sacrifice of thanksgiving, And will call on the name of Yahweh.
18 I will pay my vows to Yahweh, Yes, in the presence of all his people,
19 In the courts of Yahweh`s house, In the midst of you, Jerusalem. Praise Yah! Psalm 117

Psalms 117

1 Praise Yahweh, all you nations! Extol him, all you peoples!
2 For his lovingkindness is great toward us. Yahweh`s faithfulness endures forever. Praise Yah! Psalm 118

Psalms 118

1 Give thanks to Yahweh, for he is good, For his lovingkindness endures forever.
2 Let Israel now say That his lovingkindness endures forever.
3 Let the house of Aaron now say That his lovingkindness endures forever.

4 Now let those who fear Yahweh say That his lovingkindness endures forever.
5 Out of my distress, I called on Yah. Yah answered me with freedom.
6 Yahweh is on my side. I will not be afraid. What can man do to me?
7 Yahweh is on my side among those who help me. Therefore I will look in triumph at those who hate me.
8 It is better to take refuge in Yahweh, Than to put confidence in man.
9 It is better to take refuge in Yahweh, Than to put confidence in princes.
10 All the nations surrounded me, But in the name of Yahweh, I cut them off.
11 They surrounded me, yes, they surrounded me. In the name of Yahweh I indeed cut them off.
12 They surrounded me like bees. They are quenched like the burning thorns. In the name of Yahweh I cut them off.
13 You pushed me back hard, to make me fall, But Yahweh helped me.
14 Yah is my strength and song. He has become my salvation.
15 The voice of rejoicing and salvation is in the tents of the righteous. "The right hand of Yahweh does valiantly.
16 The right hand of Yahweh is exalted! The right hand of Yahweh does valiantly!"
17 I will not die, but live, And declare Yah`s works.
18 Yah has punished me severely, But he has not given me over to death.

[19] Open to me the gates of righteousness. I will enter into them. I will give thanks to Yah.
[20] This is the gate of Yahweh; The righteous will enter into it.
[21] I will give thanks to you, for you have answered me, And have become my salvation.
[22] The stone which the builders rejected has become the head of the corner.
[23] This is Yahweh's doing. It is marvelous in our eyes.
[24] This is the day that Yahweh has made. We will rejoice and be glad in it!
[25] Save us now, we beg you, Yahweh; Yahweh, we beg you, now send prosperity.
[26] Blessed is he who comes in the name of Yahweh! We have blessed you out of the house of Yahweh.
[27] Yahweh is God, and he has given us light. Bind the sacrifice with cords, even to the horns of the altar.
[28] You are my God, and I will give thanks to you. You are my God, I will exalt you.
[29] Oh give thanks to Yahweh, for he is good, For his lovingkindness endures forever. Psalm 119 ALEPH

Psalms 119

[1] Blessed are those whose ways are blameless, Who walk according to the law of Yahweh.

2 Blessed are those who keep his statutes, Who seek him with their whole heart.
3 Yes, they do nothing wrong. They walk in his ways.
4 You have commanded your precepts, That we should fully obey them.
5 Oh that my ways were steadfast To obey your statutes!
6 Then I wouldn`t be put to shame, When I consider all of your commandments.
7 I will give thanks to you with uprightness of heart, When I learn your righteous judgments.
8 I will observe your statutes. Don`t utterly forsake me.
BEIT
9 How can a young man keep his way pure? By living according to your word.
10 With my whole heart, I have sought you. Don`t let me wander from your commandments.
11 I have hidden your word in my heart, That I might not sin against you.
12 Blessed are you, Yahweh. Teach me your statutes.
13 With my lips, I have declared all the ordinances of your mouth.
14 I have rejoiced in the way of your testimonies, As much as in all riches.
15 I will meditate on your precepts, And consider your ways.
16 I will delight myself in your statutes. I will not forget your word. GIMEL
17 Do good to your servant. I will live and I will obey your word.

¹⁸ Open my eyes, That I may see wondrous things out of your law.
¹⁹ I am a stranger on the earth. Don`t hide your commandments from me.
²⁰ My soul is consumed with longing for your ordinances at all times.
²¹ You have rebuked the proud who are cursed, Who wander from your commandments.
²² Take reproach and contempt away from me, For I have kept your statutes.
²³ Though princes sit and slander me, Your servant will meditate on your statutes.
²⁴ Indeed your statutes are my delight, And my counselors. DALED
²⁵ My soul is laid low in the dust. Revive me according to your word!
²⁶ I declared my ways, and you answered me. Teach me your statutes.
²⁷ Let me understand the teaching of your precepts! Then I will meditate on your wondrous works.
²⁸ My soul is weary with sorrow. Strengthen me according to your word.
²⁹ Keep me from the way of deceit. Grant me your law graciously!
³⁰ I have chosen the way of truth. I have set my heart on your law.
³¹ I cling to your statutes, Yahweh. Don`t let me be put to shame.
³² I run in the path of your commandments, For you have set my heart free. HEY

33 Teach me, Yahweh, the way of your statutes. I will keep them to the end.
34 Give me understanding, and I will keep your law. Yes, I will obey it with my whole heart.
35 Direct me in the path of your commandments, For I delight in them.
36 Turn my heart toward your statutes, Not toward selfish gain.
37 Turn my eyes away from looking at worthless things. Revive me in your ways.
38 Fulfill your promise to your servant, That you may be feared.
39 Take away my disgrace that I dread, For your ordinances are good.
40 Behold, I long for your precepts! Revive me in your righteousness. WAW
41 Let your lovingkindness also come to me, Yahweh, Your salvation, according to your word.
42 So I will have an answer for him who reproaches me, For I trust in your word.
43 Don`t snatch the word of truth out of my mouth, For I put my hope in your ordinances.
44 So I will obey your law continually, Forever and ever.
45 I will walk in liberty, For I have sought your precepts.
46 I will also speak of your statutes before kings, And will not be put to shame.
47 I will delight myself in your commandments, Because I love them.
48 I reach out my hands for your commandments, which I love. I will meditate on your statutes. ZAYIN

⁴⁹ Remember your word to your servant, Because you gave me hope.
⁵⁰ This is my comfort in my affliction, For your word has revived me.
⁵¹ The arrogant mock me excessively, But I don`t swerve from your law.
⁵² I remember your ordinances of old, Yahweh, And have comforted myself.
⁵³ Indignation has taken hold on me, Because of the wicked who forsake your law.
⁵⁴ Your statutes have been my songs, In the house where I live.
⁵⁵ I have remembered your name, Yahweh, in the night, And I obey your law.
⁵⁶ This is my way, That I keep your precepts. CHET
⁵⁷ Yahweh is my portion. I promised to obey your words.
⁵⁸ I sought your favor with my whole heart. Be merciful to me according to your word.
⁵⁹ I considered my ways, And turned my steps to your statutes.
⁶⁰ I will hurry, and not delay, To obey your commandments.
⁶¹ The ropes of the wicked bind me, But I won`t forget your law.
⁶² At midnight I will rise to give thanks to you, Because of your righteous ordinances.
⁶³ I am a friend of all those who fear you, Of those who observe your precepts.
⁶⁴ The earth is full of your lovingkindness, Yahweh. Teach me your statutes. TET

⁶⁵ Do good to your servant, According to your word, Yahweh.
⁶⁶ Teach me good judgment and knowledge, For I believe in your commandments.
⁶⁷ Before I was afflicted, I went astray; But now I observe your word.
⁶⁸ You are good, and do good. Teach me your statutes.
⁶⁹ The proud have smeared a lie upon me. With my whole heart, I will keep your precepts.
⁷⁰ Their heart is as callous as the fat, But I delight in your law.
⁷¹ It is good for me that I have been afflicted, That I may learn your statutes.
⁷² The law of your mouth is better to me than thousands of pieces of gold and silver. YUD
⁷³ Your hands have made me and formed me. Give me understanding, that I may learn your commandments.
⁷⁴ Those who fear you will see me and be glad, Because I have put my hope in your word.
⁷⁵ Yahweh, I know that your judgments are righteous, That in faithfulness you have afflicted me.
⁷⁶ Please let your lovingkindness be for my comfort, According to your word to your servant.
⁷⁷ Let your tender mercies come to me, that I may live; For your law is my delight.
⁷⁸ Let the proud be put to shame, for they have overthrown me wrongfully. I will meditate on your precepts.
⁷⁹ Let those who fear you turn to me. They will know your statutes.

⁸⁰ Let my heart be blameless toward your decrees, That I may not be put to shame. KAF
⁸¹ My soul faints for your salvation. I hope in your word.
⁸² My eyes fail for your word. I say, "When will you comfort me?"
⁸³ For I have become like a wineskin in the smoke. I don`t forget your statutes.
⁸⁴ How many are the days of your servant? When will you execute judgment on those who persecute me?
⁸⁵ The proud have dug pits for me, Contrary to your law.
⁸⁶ All of your commandments are faithful. They persecute me wrongfully. Help me!
⁸⁷ They had almost wiped me from the earth, But I didn`t forsake your precepts.
⁸⁸ Preserve my life according to your lovingkindness, So I will obey the statutes of your mouth. LAMED
⁸⁹ Yahweh, your word is settled in heaven forever.
⁹⁰ Your faithfulness is to all generations. You have established the earth, and it remains.
⁹¹ Your laws remain to this day, For all things serve you.
⁹² Unless your law had been my delight, I would have perished in my affliction.
⁹³ I will never forget your precepts, For with them, you have revived me.
⁹⁴ I am yours. Save me, For I have sought your precepts.
⁹⁵ The wicked have waited for me, to destroy me. I will consider your statutes.
⁹⁶ I have seen a limit to all perfection, But your commands are boundless. MEM
⁹⁷ How love I your law! It is my meditation all day.

⁹⁸ Your commandments make me wiser than my enemies, For your commandments are always with me.
⁹⁹ I have more understanding than all my teachers, For your testimonies are my meditation.
¹⁰⁰ I understand more than the aged, Because I have kept your precepts.
¹⁰¹ I have kept my feet from every evil way, That I might observe your word.
¹⁰² I have not turned aside from your ordinances, For you have taught me.
¹⁰³ How sweet are your promises to my taste, More than honey to my mouth!
¹⁰⁴ Through your precepts, I get understanding; Therefore I hate every false way. NUN
¹⁰⁵ Your word is a lamp to my feet, And a light for my path.
¹⁰⁶ I have sworn, and have confirmed it, That I will obey your righteous ordinances.
¹⁰⁷ I am afflicted very much. Revive me, Yahweh, according to your word.
¹⁰⁸ Accept, I beg you, the willing offerings of my mouth. Yahweh, teach me your ordinances.
¹⁰⁹ My soul is continually in my hand, Yet I won't forget your law.
¹¹⁰ The wicked have laid a snare for me, Yet I haven't gone astray from your precepts.
¹¹¹ I have taken your testimonies as a heritage forever, For they are the joy of my heart.
¹¹² I have set my heart to perform your statutes forever, Even to the end. SAMEKH

¹¹³ I hate double-minded men, But I love your law.
¹¹⁴ You are my hiding place and my shield. I hope in your word.
¹¹⁵ Depart from me, you evildoers, That I may keep the commandments of my God.
¹¹⁶ Uphold me according to your word, that I may live. Let me not be ashamed of my hope.
¹¹⁷ Hold me up, and I will be safe, And will have respect for your statutes continually.
¹¹⁸ You reject all those who stray from your statutes, For their deceit is in vain.
¹¹⁹ You put away all the wicked of the earth like dross. Therefore I love your testimonies.
¹²⁰ My flesh trembles for fear of you. I am afraid of your judgments. AYIN
¹²¹ I have done what is just and righteous. Don`t leave me to my oppressors.
¹²² Ensure your servant`s well-being. Don`t let the proud oppress me.
¹²³ My eyes fail looking for your salvation, For your righteous word.
¹²⁴ Deal with your servant according to your lovingkindness. Teach me your statutes.
¹²⁵ I am your servant. Give me understanding, That I may know your testimonies.
¹²⁶ It is time to act, Yahweh, For they break your law.
¹²⁷ Therefore I love your commandments more than gold, Yes, more than pure gold.
¹²⁸ Therefore I consider all of your precepts to be right. I hate every false way. PEY

129 Your testimonies are wonderful, Therefore my soul keeps them.
130 The entrance of your words gives light. It gives understanding to the simple.
131 I opened my mouth wide and panted, For I longed for your commandments.
132 Turn to me, and have mercy on me, As you always do to those who love your name.
133 Establish my footsteps in your word. Don't let any iniquity have dominion over me.
134 Redeem me from the oppression of man, So I will observe your precepts.
135 Make your face to shine on your servant. Teach me your statutes.
136 Streams of tears run down my eyes, Because they don't observe your law. TZADI
137 You are righteous, Yahweh. your judgments are upright.
138 You have commanded your statutes in righteousness. They are fully trustworthy.
139 My zeal wears me out, Because my enemies ignore your words.
140 Your promises have been thoroughly tested, And your servant loves them.
141 I am small and despised. I don't forget your precepts.
142 Your righteousness is an everlasting righteousness. Your law is truth.
143 Trouble and anguish have taken hold of me. Your commandments are my delight.

¹⁴⁴ Your testimonies are righteous forever. Give me understanding, that I may live. KUF
¹⁴⁵ I have called with my whole heart. Answer me, Yahweh! I will keep your statutes.
¹⁴⁶ I have called to you. Save me! I will obey your statutes.
¹⁴⁷ I rise before dawn and cry for help. I put my hope in your words.
¹⁴⁸ My eyes stay open through the night watches, That I might meditate on your word.
¹⁴⁹ Hear my voice according to your lovingkindness. Revive me, Yahweh, according to your ordinances.
¹⁵⁰ They draw near who follow after wickedness. They are far from your law.
¹⁵¹ You are near, Yahweh. All your commandments are truth.
¹⁵² Of old I have known from your testimonies, That you have founded them forever. RESH
¹⁵³ Consider my affliction, and deliver me, For I don`t forget your law.
¹⁵⁴ Plead my cause, and redeem me! Revive me according to your promise.
¹⁵⁵ Salvation is far from the wicked, For they don`t seek your statutes.
¹⁵⁶ Great are your tender mercies, Yahweh. Revive me according to your ordinances.
¹⁵⁷ Many are my persecutors and my adversaries. I haven`t swerved from your testimonies.
¹⁵⁸ I look at the faithless with loathing, Because they don`t observe your word.

¹⁵⁹ Consider how I love your precepts. Revive me, Yahweh, according to your lovingkindness.
¹⁶⁰ All of your words are truth. Every one of your righteous ordinances endures forever. SIN AND SHIN
¹⁶¹ Princes have persecuted me without a cause, But my heart stands in awe of your words.
¹⁶² I rejoice at your word, As one who finds great spoil.
¹⁶³ I hate and abhor falsehood. I love your law.
¹⁶⁴ Seven times a day, I praise you, Because of your righteous ordinances.
¹⁶⁵ Those who love your law have great peace. Nothing causes them to stumble.
¹⁶⁶ I have hoped for your salvation, Yahweh. I have done your commandments.
¹⁶⁷ My soul has observed your testimonies. I love them exceedingly.
¹⁶⁸ I have obeyed your precepts and your testimonies, For all my ways are before you. TAV
¹⁶⁹ Let my cry come before you, Yahweh. Give me understanding according to your word.
¹⁷⁰ Let my supplication come before you. Deliver me according to your word.
¹⁷¹ Let my lips utter praise, For you teach me your statutes.
¹⁷² Let my tongue sing of your word, For all your commandments are righteousness.
¹⁷³ Let your hand be ready to help me, For I have chosen your precepts.
¹⁷⁴ I have longed for your salvation, Yahweh. Your law is my delight.

¹⁷⁵ Let my soul live, that I may praise you. Let your ordinances help me.
¹⁷⁶ I have gone astray like a lost sheep. Seek your servant, for I don`t forget your commandments. Psalm 120 A Song of Ascents.

Psalms 120

¹ In my distress, I cried to Yahweh. He answered me.
² Deliver my soul, Yahweh, from lying lips, From a deceitful tongue.
³ What will be given to you, and what will be done more to you, You deceitful tongue?
⁴ Sharp arrows of the mighty, With coals of juniper.
⁵ Woe is me, that I live in Meshech, That I dwell among the tents of Kedar!
⁶ My soul has had her dwelling too long With him who hates peace.
⁷ I am for peace, But when I speak, they are for war. Psalm 121 A Song of Ascents.

Psalms 121

¹ I will lift up my eyes to the hills. Where does my help come from?
² My help comes from Yahweh, Who made heaven and earth.

³ He will not allow your foot to be moved. He who keeps you will not slumber.
⁴ Behold, he who keeps Israel Will neither slumber nor sleep.
⁵ Yahweh is your keeper. Yahweh is your shade on your right hand.
⁶ The sun will not harm you by day, Nor the moon by night.
⁷ Yahweh will keep you from all evil. He will keep your soul.
⁸ Yahweh will keep your going out and your coming in, From this time forth, and forevermore. Psalm 122 A Song of Ascents. By David.

Psalms 122

¹ I was glad when they said to me, "Let`s go to Yahweh`s house!"
² Our feet are standing Within your gates, Jerusalem;
³ Jerusalem, that is built As a city that is compact together;
⁴ Where the tribes go up, even Yah`s tribes, According to an ordinance for Israel, To give thanks to the name of Yahweh.
⁵ For there are set thrones for judgment, The thrones of David`s house.
⁶ Pray for the peace of Jerusalem. They will prosper who love you.

⁷ Peace be within your walls, And prosperity within your palaces.
⁸ For my brothers` and companions` sakes, I will now say, "Peace be within you."
⁹ For the sake of the house of Yahweh our God, I will seek your good. Psalm 123 A Song of Ascents.

Psalms 123

¹ To you I do lift up my eyes, You who sit in the heavens.
² Behold, as the eyes of servants look to the hand of their master, As the eyes of a maid to the hand of her mistress; So our eyes look to Yahweh, our God, Until he has mercy on us.
³ Have mercy on us, Yahweh, have mercy on us, For we have endured much contempt.
⁴ Our soul is exceedingly filled with the scoffing of those who are at ease, With the contempt of the proud. Psalm 124 A Song of Ascents. By David.

Psalms 124

¹ If it had not been Yahweh who was on our side, Let Israel now say,
² If it had not been Yahweh who was on our side, When men rose up against us;

³ Then they would have swallowed us up alive, When their wrath was kindled against us;
⁴ Then the waters would have overwhelmed us, The stream would have gone over our soul;
⁵ Then the proud waters would have gone over our soul.
⁶ Blessed be Yahweh, Who has not given us as a prey to their teeth.
⁷ Our soul has escaped like a bird out of the fowler's snare. The snare is broken, and we have escaped.
⁸ Our help is in the name of Yahweh, Who made heaven and earth. Psalm 125 A Song of Ascents.

Psalms 125

¹ Those who trust in Yahweh are as Mount Zion, Which can't be moved, but remains forever.
² As the mountains surround Jerusalem, So Yahweh surrounds his people from this time forth and forevermore.
³ For the scepter of wickedness won't remain over the allotment of the righteous; So that the righteous won't put forth their hands to iniquity.
⁴ Do good, Yahweh, to those who are good, To those who are upright in their hearts.
⁵ But as for those who turn aside to their crooked ways, Yahweh will lead them away with the workers of

iniquity. Peace be on Israel. Psalm 126 A Song of Ascents.

Psalms 126

¹ When Yahweh brought back those who returned to Zion, We were like those who dream.
² Then our mouth was filled with laughter, And our tongue with singing. Then said they among the nations, "Yahweh has done great things for them."
³ Yahweh has done great things for us, And we are glad.
⁴ Restore our fortunes again, Yahweh, Like the streams in the Negev.
⁵ Those who sow in tears will reap in joy.
⁶ He who goes out weeping, carrying seed for sowing, Will assuredly come again with joy, carrying his sheaves. Psalm 127 A Song of Ascents. By Solomon.

Psalms 127

¹ Unless Yahweh builds the house, They labor in vain who build it. Unless Yahweh watches over the city, The watchman guards it in vain.
² It is vain for you to rise up early, To stay up late, Eating the bread of toil; For he gives sleep to his loved ones.
³ Behold, children are a heritage of Yahweh. The fruit of the womb is his reward.

⁴ As arrows in the hand of a mighty man, So are the children of youth.
⁵ Happy is the man who has his quiver full of them. They won't be put to shame when they speak with their enemies in the gate. Psalm 128 A Song of Ascents.

Psalms 128

¹ Blessed is everyone who fears Yahweh, Who walks in his ways.
² For you will eat the labor of your hands. You will be happy, and it will be well with you.
³ Your wife will be as a fruitful vine, In the innermost parts of your house; Your children like olive plants, Around your table.
⁴ Behold, thus is the man blessed who fears Yahweh.
⁵ May Yahweh bless you out of Zion, And may you see the good of Jerusalem all the days of your life.
⁶ Yes, may you see your children's children. Peace be upon Israel. Psalm 129 A Song of Ascents.

Psalms 129

¹ Many times have they afflicted me from my youth up. Let Israel now say,
² Many times have they afflicted me from my youth up, Yet they have not prevailed against me.

³ The plowers plowed on my back. They made their furrows long.
⁴ Yahweh is righteous. He has cut apart the cords of the wicked.
⁵ Let them be put to shame and turned backward, All those who hate Zion.
⁶ Let them be as the grass on the housetops, Which withers before it grows up;
⁷ With which the reaper doesn't fill his hand, Nor he who binds sheaves, his bosom.
⁸ Neither do those who go by say, "The blessing of Yahweh be on you. We bless you in the name of Yahweh." Psalm 130 A Song of Ascents.

Psalms 130

¹ Out of the depths I have cried to you, Yahweh.
² Lord, hear my voice. Let your ears be attentive to the voice of my petitions.
³ If you, Yah, kept a record of sins, Lord, who could stand?
⁴ But there is forgiveness with you, Therefore you are feared.
⁵ I wait for Yahweh. My soul waits. I hope in his word.
⁶ My soul longs for the Lord more than watchmen long for the morning; More than watchmen for the morning.
⁷ Israel, hope in Yahweh, For with Yahweh there is lovingkindness. With him is abundant redemption.

⁸ He will redeem Israel from all their sins. Psalm 131 A Song of Ascents. By David.

Psalms 131

¹ Yahweh, my heart isn`t haughty, nor my eyes lofty; Neither do I concern myself with great matters, Or things too wonderful for me.
² Surely I have stilled and quieted my soul, Like a weaned child with his mother, Like a weaned child is my soul within me.
³ Israel, hope in Yahweh, From this time forth and forevermore. Psalm 132 A Song of Ascents.

Psalms 132

¹ Yahweh, remember David and all his affliction,
² How he swore to Yahweh, And vowed to the Mighty One of Jacob:
³ "Surely I will not come into the structure of my house, Nor go up into my bed;
⁴ I will not give sleep to my eyes, Or slumber to my eyelids;
⁵ Until I find out a place for Yahweh, A dwelling for the Mighty One of Jacob."

⁶ Behold, we heard of it in Ephrathah. We found it in the field of Jaar:
⁷ "We will go into his dwelling place. We will worship at his footstool.
⁸ Arise, Yahweh, into your resting place; You, and the ark of your strength.
⁹ Let your priest be clothed with righteousness. Let your saints shout for joy!"
¹⁰ For your servant David's sake, Don't turn away the face of your anointed one.
¹¹ Yahweh has sworn to David in truth. He will not turn from it: "I will set the fruit of your body on your throne.
¹² If your children will keep my covenant, My testimony that I will teach them, Their children also will sit on your throne forevermore."
¹³ For Yahweh has chosen Zion. He has desired it for his habitation.
¹⁴ "This is my resting place forever. Here I will live, for I have desired it.
¹⁵ I will abundantly bless her provision. I will satisfy her poor with bread.
¹⁶ Her priests I will also clothe with salvation. Her saints will shout aloud for joy.
¹⁷ There I will make the horn of David to bud. I have ordained a lamp for my anointed.
¹⁸ I will clothe his enemies with shame, But on himself, his crown will be resplendant." Psalm 133 A Song of Ascents. By David.

Psalms 133

¹ See how good and how pleasant it is for brothers to live together in unity!
² It is like the precious oil on the head, That ran down on the beard, Even Aaron`s beard; That came down on the edge of his robes;
³ Like the dew of Hermon, That comes down on the hills of Zion: For there Yahweh gives the blessing, Even life forevermore. Psalm 134 A Song of Ascents.

Psalms 134

¹ Look! Praise Yahweh, all you servants of Yahweh, Who stand by night in Yahweh`s house!
² Lift up your hands in the sanctuary. Praise Yahweh!
³ May Yahweh bless you from Zion; Even he who made heaven and earth. Psalm 135

Psalms 135

¹ Praise Yah! Praise the name of Yahweh! Praise him, you servants of Yahweh,
² You who stand in the house of Yahweh, In the courts of our God`s house.

³ Praise Yah, for Yahweh is good. Sing praises to his name, for that is pleasant.
⁴ For Yah has chosen Jacob for himself; Israel for his own possession.
⁵ For I know that Yahweh is great, That our Lord is above all gods.
⁶ Whatever Yahweh pleased, that he has done, In heaven and in earth, in the seas and in all deeps;
⁷ Who causes the clouds to rise from the ends of the earth; Who makes lightnings with the rain; Who brings forth the wind out of his treasuries;
⁸ Who struck the firstborn of Egypt, Both of man and animal;
⁹ Who sent signs and wonders into the midst of you, Egypt, On Pharaoh, and on all his servants;
¹⁰ Who struck many nations, And killed mighty kings,
¹¹ Sihon king of the Amorites, Og king of Bashan, All the kingdoms of Canaan,
¹² And gave their land for a heritage, A heritage to Israel, his people.
¹³ Your name, Yahweh, endures forever; Your renown, Yahweh, throughout all generations.
¹⁴ For Yahweh will judge his people, And have compassion on his servants.
¹⁵ The idols of the nations are silver and gold, The work of men`s hands.
¹⁶ They have mouths, but they can`t speak; They have eyes, but they can`t see;
¹⁷ They have ears, but they can`t hear; Neither is there any breath in their mouths.

18 Those who make them will be like them; Yes, everyone who trusts in them.
19 House of Israel, praise Yahweh! House of Aaron, praise Yahweh!
20 House of Levi, praise Yahweh! You who fear Yahweh, praise Yahweh!
21 Blessed be Yahweh from Zion, Who dwells at Jerusalem. Praise Yah! Psalm 136

Psalms 136

1 Give thanks to Yahweh, for he is good; For his lovingkindness endures forever.
2 Give thanks to the God of gods; For his lovingkindness endures forever.
3 Give thanks to the Lord of lords; For his lovingkindness endures forever:
4 To him who alone does great wonders; For his lovingkindness endures forever:
5 To him who by understanding made the heavens; For his lovingkindness endures forever:
6 To him who spread out the earth above the waters; For his lovingkindness endures forever:
7 To him who made the great lights; For his lovingkindness endures forever:
8 The sun to rule by day; For his lovingkindness endures forever;

⁹ The moon and stars to rule by night; For his lovingkindness endures forever:
¹⁰ To him who struck down the Egyptian firstborn; For his lovingkindness endures forever;
¹¹ And brought out Israel from among them; For his lovingkindness endures forever;
¹² With a strong hand, and with an outstretched arm; For his lovingkindness endures forever:
¹³ To him who divided the Red Sea apart; For his lovingkindness endures forever;
¹⁴ Made Israel to pass through the midst of it; For his lovingkindness endures forever;
¹⁵ But overthrew Pharaoh and his host in the Red Sea; For his lovingkindness endures forever:
¹⁶ To him who led his people through the wilderness; For his lovingkindness endures forever:
¹⁷ To him who struck great kings; For his lovingkindness endures forever;
¹⁸ And killed mighty kings; For his lovingkindness endures forever:
¹⁹ Sihon king of the Amorites; For his lovingkindness endures forever;
²⁰ Og king of Bashan; For his lovingkindness endures forever;
²¹ And gave their land as an inheritance; For his lovingkindness endures forever;
²² Even a heritage to Israel his servant; For his lovingkindness endures forever:
²³ Who remembered us in our low estate; For his lovingkindness endures forever;

24 And has delivered us from our adversaries; For his lovingkindness endures forever:
25 Who gives food to every creature; For his lovingkindness endures forever.
26 Oh give thanks to the God of heaven; For his lovingkindness endures forever.

Psalms 137

1 By the rivers of Babylon, there we sat down. Yes, we wept, when we remembered Zion.
2 On the willows in the midst of it, We hung up our harps.
3 For there, those who led us captive asked us for songs. Those who tormented us demanded songs of joy: "Sing us one of the songs of Zion!"
4 How can we sing Yahweh`s song in a foreign land?
5 If I forget you, Jerusalem, Let my right hand forget its skill.
6 Let my tongue stick to the roof of my mouth, If I don`t remember you; If I don`t prefer Jerusalem above my chief joy.
7 Remember, Yahweh, against the children of Edom, The day of Jerusalem; Who said, "Raze it! Raze it even to its foundation!"
8 Daughter of Babylon, doomed to destruction, He will be happy who rewards you, As you have served us.
9 Happy shall he be, Who takes and dashes your little ones against the rock. Psalm 138 By David.

Psalms 138

¹ I will give you thanks with my whole heart. Before the gods, I will sing praises to you.
² I will bow down toward your holy temple, And give thanks to your Name for your lovingkindness and for your truth; For you have exalted your Name and your Word above all.
³ In the day that I called, you answered me. You encouraged me with strength in my soul.
⁴ All the kings of the earth will give you thanks, Yahweh, For they have heard the words of your mouth.
⁵ Yes, they will sing of the ways of Yahweh; For great is Yahweh's glory.
⁶ For though Yahweh is high, yet he looks after the lowly; But the proud, he knows from afar.
⁷ Though I walk in the midst of trouble, you will revive me. You will stretch forth your hand against the wrath of my enemies. Your right hand will save me.
⁸ Yahweh will fulfill that which concerns me; Your lovingkindness, Yahweh, endures forever. Don't forsake the works of your own hands. Psalm 139 For the Chief Musician. A Psalm by David.

Psalms 139

¹ Yahweh, you have searched me, And you know me.

² You know my sitting down and my rising up. You perceive my thoughts from afar.
³ You search out my path and my lying down, And are acquainted with all my ways.
⁴ For there is not a word on my tongue, But, behold, Yahweh, you know it altogether.
⁵ You hem me in behind and before. You laid your hand on me.
⁶ This knowledge is beyond me. It is lofty. I can`t attain it.
⁷ Where could I go from your Spirit? Or where could I flee from your presence?
⁸ If I ascend up into heaven, you are there. If I make my bed in Sheol, behold, you are there!
⁹ If I take the wings of the dawn, And settle in the uttermost parts of the sea;
¹⁰ Even there your hand will lead me, And your right hand will hold me.
¹¹ If I say, "Surely the darkness will overwhelm me; The light around me will be night;"
¹² Even the darkness doesn`t hide from you, But the night shines as the day. The darkness is like light to you.
¹³ For you formed my inmost being. You knit me together in my mother`s womb.
¹⁴ I will give thanks to you, For I am fearfully and wonderfully made. Your works are wonderful. My soul knows that very well.
¹⁵ My frame wasn`t hidden from you, When I was made in secret, Woven together in the depths of the earth.

¹⁶ Your eyes saw my body. In your book they were all written, The days that were ordained for me, When as yet there were none of them.
¹⁷ How precious to me are your thoughts, God! How vast is the sum of them!
¹⁸ If I would count them, they are more in number than the sand. When I wake up, I am still with you.
¹⁹ If only you, God, would kill the wicked. Get away from me, you bloodthirsty men!
²⁰ For they speak against you wickedly. Your enemies take your name in vain.
²¹ Yahweh, don`t I hate those who hate you? Am I not grieved with those who rise up against you?
²² I hate them with perfect hatred. They have become my enemies.
²³ Search me, God, and know my heart. Try me, and know my thoughts.
²⁴ See if there is any wicked way in me, And lead me in the everlasting way. Psalm 140 For the Chief Musician. A Psalm by David.

Psalms 140

¹ Deliver me, Yahweh, from the evil man. Preserve me from the violent man;
² Those who devise mischief in their hearts. They continually gather themselves together for war.

3 They have sharpened their tongues like a serpent. Viper's poison is under their lips. Selah.
4 Yahweh, keep me from the hands of the wicked. Preserve me from the violent men: Who have determined to trip my feet.
5 The proud have hidden a snare for me, They have spread the cords of a net by the path. They have set traps for me. Selah.
6 I said to Yahweh, "You are my God." Listen to the cry of my petitions, Yahweh.
7 Yahweh, the Lord, the strength of my salvation, You have covered my head in the day of battle.
8 Yahweh, don't grant the desires of the wicked. Don't let their evil plans succeed, or they will become proud. Selah.
9 As for the head of those who surround me, Let the mischief of their own lips cover them.
10 Let burning coals fall on them. Let them be thrown into the fire, Into miry pits, from where they never rise.
11 An evil speaker won't be established in the earth. Evil will hunt the violent man to overthrow him.
12 I know that Yahweh will maintain the cause of the afflicted, And justice for the needy.
13 Surely the righteous will give thanks to your name. The upright will dwell in your presence. Psalm 141 A Psalm by David.

Psalms 141

¹ Yahweh, I have called on you. Come to me quickly! Listen to my voice when I call to you.
² Let my prayer be set before you like incense; The lifting up of my hands like the evening sacrifice.
³ Set a watch, Yahweh, before my mouth. Keep the door of my lips.
⁴ Don`t incline my heart to any evil thing, To practice deeds of wickedness with men who work iniquity. Don`t let me eat of their delicacies.
⁵ Let the righteous strike me, it is kindness; Let him reprove me, it is like oil on the head; Don`t let my head refuse it; Yet my prayer is always against evil deeds.
⁶ Their judges are thrown down by the sides of the rock. They will hear my words, for they are well spoken.
⁷ "As when one plows and breaks up the earth, Our bones are scattered at the mouth of Sheol."
⁸ For my eyes are on you, Yahweh, the Lord. In you, I take refuge. Don`t leave my soul destitute.
⁹ Keep me from the snare which they have laid for me, From the traps of the workers of iniquity.
¹⁰ Let the wicked fall together into their own nets, While I pass by. Psalm 142 A contemplation by David, when he was in the cave. A Prayer.

Psalms 142

¹ I cry with my voice to Yahweh. With my voice, I ask Yahweh for mercy.
² I pour out my complaint before him. I tell him my troubles.
³ When my spirit was overwhelmed within me, You knew my path. In the way in which I walk, They have hidden a snare for me.
⁴ Look on my right, and see; For there is no one who is concerned for me. Refuge has fled from me. No one cares for my soul.
⁵ I cried to you, Yahweh. I said, "You are my refuge, My portion in the land of the living."
⁶ Listen to my cry, For I am in desperate need. Deliver me from my persecutors, For they are stronger than me.
⁷ Bring my soul out of prison, That I may give thanks to your name. The righteous will surround me, For you will be good to me. Psalm 143 A Psalm by David.

Psalms 143

¹ Hear my prayer, Yahweh. Listen to my petitions. In your faithfulness and righteousness, relieve me.
² Don`t enter into judgment with your servant, For in your sight no man living is righteous.
³ For the enemy pursues my soul. He has struck my life down to the ground. He has made me live in dark places, as those who have been long dead.

⁴ Therefore my spirit is overwhelmed within me. My heart within me is desolate.
⁵ I remember the days of old. I meditate on all your doings. I contemplate the work of your hands.
⁶ I spread forth my hands to you. My soul thirsts for you, like a parched land. Selah.
⁷ Hurry to answer me, Yahweh. My spirit fails. Don`t hide your face from me, So that I don`t become like those who go down into the pit.
⁸ Cause me to hear your lovingkindness in the morning, For I trust in you. Cause me to know the way in which I should walk, For I lift up my soul to you.
⁹ Deliver me, Yahweh, from my enemies. I flee to you to hide me.
¹⁰ Teach me to do your will, For you are my God. Your Spirit is good. Lead me in the land of uprightness.
¹¹ Revive me, Yahweh, for your name`s sake. In your righteousness, bring my soul out of trouble.
¹² In your lovingkindness, cut off my enemies, And destroy all those who afflict my soul, For I am your servant. Psalm 144 By David.

Psalms 144

¹ Blessed be Yahweh, my rock, Who teaches my hands to war, And my fingers to battle:

² My lovingkindness, my fortress, My high tower, my deliverer, My shield, and he in whom I take refuge; Who subdues my people under me.
³ Yahweh, what is man, that you care for him? Or the son of man, that you think of him?
⁴ Man is like a breath. His days are like a shadow that passes away.
⁵ Part your heavens, Yahweh, and come down. Touch the mountains, and they will smoke.
⁶ Throw out lightning, and scatter them. Send out your arrows, and rout them.
⁷ Stretch out your hand from above, Rescue me, and deliver me out of great waters, Out of the hands of foreigners;
⁸ Whose mouths speak deceit, Whose right hand is a right hand of falsehood.
⁹ I will sing a new song to you, God. On a ten-stringed lyre, I will sing praises to you.
¹⁰ You are he who gives salvation to kings, Who rescues David, his servant, from the deadly sword.
¹¹ Rescue me, and deliver me out of the hands of foreigners, Whose mouths speak deceit, Whose right hand is a right hand of falsehood.
¹² Then our sons will be like well-nurtured plants, Our daughters like pillars carved to adorn a palace.
¹³ Our barns are full, filled with all kinds of provision. Our sheep bring forth thousands and ten thousands in our fields.
¹⁴ Our oxen will pull heavy loads. There is no breaking in, and no going away, And no outcry in our streets.

¹⁵ Happy are the people who are in such a situation. Happy are the people whose God is Yahweh. Psalm 145 A praise psalm by David.

Psalms 145

¹ I will exalt you, my God, the King. I will praise your name forever and ever.
² Every day I will praise you. I will extol your name forever and ever.
³ Great is Yahweh, and greatly to be praised! His greatness is unsearchable.
⁴ One generation will commend your works to another, And will declare your mighty acts.
⁵ Of the glorious majesty of your honor, Of your wondrous works, I will meditate.
⁶ Men will speak of the might of your awesome acts. I will declare your greatness.
⁷ They will utter the memory of your great goodness, And will sing of your righteousness.
⁸ Yahweh is gracious, merciful, Slow to anger, and of great lovingkindness.
⁹ Yahweh is good to all. His tender mercies are over all his works.
¹⁰ All your works will give thanks to you, Yahweh. Your saints will extol you.

11 They will speak of the glory of your kingdom, And talk about your power;
12 To make known to the sons of men his mighty acts, The glory of the majesty of his kingdom.
13 Your kingdom is an everlasting kingdom. Your dominion endures throughout all generations.
14 Yahweh upholds all who fall, And raises up all those who are bowed down.
15 The eyes of all wait for you. You give them their food in due season.
16 You open your hand, And satisfy the desire of every living thing.
17 Yahweh is righteous in all his ways, And gracious in all his works.
18 Yahweh is near to all those who call on him, To all who call on him in truth.
19 He will fulfill the desire of those who fear him. He also will hear their cry, and will save them.
20 Yahweh preserves all those who love him, But all the wicked he will destroy.
21 My mouth will speak the praise of Yahweh. Let all flesh bless his holy name forever and ever. Psalm 146

Psalms 146

1 Praise Yah! Praise Yahweh, my soul.
2 While I live, I will praise Yahweh. I will sing praises to my God as long as I exist.

³ Don't put your trust in princes, Each a son of man in whom there is no help.
⁴ His spirit departs, and he returns to the earth. In that very day, his thoughts perish.
⁵ Happy is he who has the God of Jacob for his help, Whose hope is in Yahweh, his God:
⁶ Who made heaven and earth, The sea, and all that is in them; Who keeps truth forever;
⁷ Who executes justice for the oppressed; Who gives food to the hungry. Yahweh frees the prisoners.
⁸ Yahweh opens the eyes of the blind. Yahweh raises up those who are bowed down. Yahweh loves the righteous.
⁹ Yahweh preserves the sojourners. He upholds the fatherless and widow, But the way of the wicked he turns upside down.
¹⁰ Yahweh will reign forever; Your God, O Zion, to all generations. Praise Yah! Psalm 147

Psalms 147

¹ Praise Yah, For it is good to sing praises to our God; For it is pleasant and fitting to praise him.
² Yahweh builds up Jerusalem. He gathers together the outcasts of Israel.
³ He heals the broken in heart, And binds up their wounds.
⁴ He counts the number of the stars. He calls them all by their names.

5 Great is our Lord, and mighty in power. His understanding is infinite.
6 Yahweh upholds the humble. He brings the wicked down to the ground.
7 Sing to Yahweh with thanksgiving. Sing praises on the harp to our God,
8 Who covers the sky with clouds, Who prepares rain for the earth, Who makes grass grow on the mountains.
9 He provides food for the cattle, And for the young ravens when they call.
10 He doesn`t delight in the strength of the horse. He takes no pleasure in the legs of a man.
11 Yahweh takes pleasure in those who fear him, In those who hope in his lovingkindness.
12 Praise Yahweh, Jerusalem! Praise your God, Zion!
13 For he has strengthened the bars of your gates. He has blessed your children within you.
14 He makes peace in your borders. He fills you with the finest of the wheat.
15 He sends out his commandment on earth. His word runs very swiftly.
16 He gives snow like wool, And scatters frost like ashes.
17 He hurls down his hail like pebbles. Who can stand before his cold?
18 He sends out his word, and melts them. He causes his wind to blow, and the waters flow.
19 He shows his word to Jacob; His statutes and his ordinances to Israel.
20 He has not done this for any nation; They don`t know his ordinances. Praise Yah! Psalm 148

Psalms 148

¹ Praise Yah! Praise Yahweh from the heavens! Praise him in the heights!
² Praise him, all his angels! Praise him, all his host!
³ Praise him, sun and moon! Praise him, all you shining stars!
⁴ Praise him, you heavens of heavens, You waters that are above the heavens.
⁵ Let them praise the name of Yahweh, For he commanded, and they were created.
⁶ He has also established them forever and ever. He has made a decree which will not pass away.
⁷ Praise Yahweh from the earth, You great sea creatures, and all depths!
⁸ Lightning and hail, snow and clouds; Stormy wind, fulfilling his word;
⁹ Mountains and all hills; Fruit trees and all cedars;
¹⁰ Wild animals and all cattle; Small creatures and flying birds;
¹¹ Kings of the earth and all peoples; Princes and all judges of the earth;
¹² Both young men and maidens; Old men and children:
¹³ Let them praise the name of Yahweh, For his name alone is exalted. His glory is above the earth and the heavens.

¹⁴ He has lifted up the horn of his people, The praise of all his saints; Even of the children of Israel, a people near to him. Praise Yah! Psalm 149

Psalms 149

¹ Praise Yahweh! Sing to Yahweh a new song, His praise in the assembly of the saints.
² Let Israel rejoice in him who made them. Let the children of Zion be joyful in their King.
³ Let them praise his name in the dance! Let them sing praises to him with tambourine and harp!
⁴ For Yahweh takes pleasure in his people. He crowns the humble with salvation.
⁵ Let the saints rejoice in honor. Let them sing for joy on their beds.
⁶ May the high praises of God be in their mouths, And a two-edged sword in their hand;
⁷ To execute vengeance on the nations, And punishments on the peoples;
⁸ To bind their kings with chains, And their nobles with fetters of iron;
⁹ To execute on them the written judgment. All his saints have this honor. Praise Yah! Psalm 150

Psalms 150

¹ Praise Yah! Praise God in his sanctuary! Praise him in his heavens for his acts of power!
² Praise him for his mighty acts! Praise him according to his excellent greatness!
³ Praise him with the sounding of the trumpet! Praise him with harp and lyre!
⁴ Praise him with tambourine and dancing! Praise him with stringed instruments and flute!
⁵ Praise him with loud cymbals! Praise him with resounding cymbals!
⁶ Let everything that has breath praise Yah! Praise Yah!

www.ingramcontent.com/pod-product-compliance
Lightning Source LLC
Chambersburg PA
CBHW060831220526
45466CB00003B/1067